Idea, The Shepherds Garland by Michael Drayton

Fashioned in Nine Eglogs. Rowlands Sacrifice to the Nine Muses.

Michael Drayton was born in 1563 at Hartshill, near Nuneaton, Warwickshire, England. The facts of his early life remain unknown.

Drayton first published, in 1590, a volume of spiritual poems; The Harmony of the Church. Ironically the Archbishop of Canterbury seized almost the entire edition and had it destroyed.

In 1593 he published Idea: The Shepherd's Garland, 9 pastorals celebrating his own love-sorrows under the poetic name of Rowland. This was later expanded to a 64 sonnet cycle.

With the publication of The Legend of Piers Gaveston, Matilda and Mortimeriados, later enlarged and re-published, in 1603, under the title of The Barons' Wars. His career began to gather interest and attention.

In 1596, The Legend of Robert, Duke of Normandy, another historical poem was published, followed in 1597 by England's Heroical Epistles, a series of historical studies, in imitation of those of Ovid. Written in the heroic couplet, they contain some of his finest writing.

Like other poets of his era, Drayton wrote for the theatre; but unlike Shakespeare, Jonson, or Samuel Daniel, he invested little of his art in the genre. Between 1597 and 1602, Drayton was a member of the stable of playwrights who worked for Philip Henslowe. Henslowe's Diary links Drayton's name with 23 plays from that period, and, for all but one unfinished work, in collaboration with others such as Thomas Dekker, Anthony Munday, and Henry Chettle. Only one play has survived; Part 1 of Sir John Oldcastle, which Drayton wrote with Munday, Robert Wilson, and Richard Hathwaye but little of Drayton can be seen in its pages.

By this time, as a poet, Drayton was well received and admired at the Court of Elizabeth 1st. If he hoped to continue that admiration with the accession of James 1st he thought wrong. In 1603, he addressed a poem of compliment to James I, but it was ridiculed, and his services rudely rejected.

In 1605 Drayton reprinted his most important works; the historical poems and the Idea. Also published was a fantastic satire called The Man in the Moon and, for the for the first time the famous Ballad of Agincourt.

Since 1598 he had worked on Poly-Olbion, a work to celebrate all the points of topographical or antiquarian interest in Great Britain. Eighteen books in total, the first were published in 1614 and the last in 1622.

In 1627 he published another of his miscellaneous volumes. In it Drayton printed The Battle of Agincourt (an historical poem but not to be confused with his ballad on the same subject), The Miseries of Queen Margaret, and the acclaimed Nimphidia, the Court of Faery, as well as several other important pieces.

Drayton last published in 1630 with The Muses' Elizium.

Michael Drayton died in London on December 23rd, 1631. He was buried in Westminster Abbey, in Poets' Corner. A monument was placed there with memorial lines attributed to Ben Jonson.

Index of Contents

DEDICATION

TO THE NOBLE, AND VALEROUS GENTLEMAN, MASTER ROBERT DUDLEY: ENRICHED WITH ALL VERTVES OF THE MINDE, AND WORTHY OF ALL HONORA|BLE DESERT.

Your most affectionate, and devoted:
Michael Drayton.

THE FIRST EGLOG.

When as the joyfull spring brings in the Summers sweete reliefe:
Poore Rowland malcontent be wayles the winter of his griefe.

Now Phoebus from the equinoctiall Zone,
Had task'd his teame vnto the higher spheare.
And from the brightnes of his glorious throne,
Sends forth his Beames to light the lower ayre,
The cheerfull welkin, comen this long look'd hower,
Distils adowne full many a silver shower.

Fayre Philomel night-musicke of the spring,
Sweetly recordes her tunefull harmony,
And with deepe sobbes, and dolefull sorrowing,

Before fayre Cinthya actes her Tragedy:
The Throstle cock, by breaking of the day,
Chants to his sweete, full many a lovely lay.

The crawling snake, against the morning sunne,
Now streaks him in his rayn-bow coloured cote:
The darkesome shades, as loathsome he doth shunne,
Inchanted with the Birds sweete silvan note:
The Buck forsakes the launds where he hath fed,
And scornes the hunt should view his velvet head.

Through all the partes, dispersed is the blood,
The lustie spring, in flower of all her pride,
Man, bird, and beast, and fish, in pleasant flood,
Rejoycing all in this most joyfull tide:
Saue Rowland leaning on a Ranpick tree,
O'r growne with age, forlorne with woe was he.

Oh blessed Pan, thou shepheards god sayth he,
O thou Creator of the starrie light,
Whose wonderous workes shew thy divinitie,
Thou wise inuentor of the day and night,
Refreshing nature with the lovely spring,
Quite blemisht erst, with stormy winters sting.

O thou strong builder of the firmament,
Who placedst Phoebus in his fierie Carre,
And by thy mighty Godhead didst inuent,
The planets mansions that they should not iarre,
Ordeyning Phebe, mistresse of the night,
From Tytans flame to steale her forked light.

Even from the cleerest christall shining throne,
Vnder whose feete the heauens are low abased,
Commaunding in thy maiestie alone,
Whereas the fiery Cherubines are placed:
Receiue my vowes as incense vnto thee,
My tribute due to thy eternitie.

O shepheards soueraigne, yea receiue in gree,
The gushing teares, from never-resting eyes,
And let those prayers which I shall make to thee,
Be in thy sight perfumed sacrifice:
Let smokie sighes be pledges of contrition,
For follies past to make my soules submission.

Submission makes amends for all my misse,
Contrition a refined life begins,

Then sacred sighes, what thing more precious is?
And prayers be oblations for my sinnes,
Repentant teares, from heauen-beholding eyes,
Ascend the ayre, and penetrate the skies.

My sorowes waxe, my joyes are in the wayning,
My hope decayes, and my despayre is springing,
My love hath losse, and my disgrace hath gayning,
Wrong rules, desert with teares her hands sits wringing:
Sorrow, despayre, disgrace, and wrong, doe thwart
My Joy, my love, my hope, and my desert.

Deuouring time shall swallow up my sorrowes,
And strong beliefe shall torture black despaire,
Death shall orewhelme disgrace, in deepest furrowes,
And Iustice laie my wrongs upon the Beere:
Thus Iustice, death, beleefe, and time, ere long,
Shall end my woes, despayre, disgrace, and wrong.

Yet time shall be expir'd and lose his date,
And full assurance cancell strongest trust,
Eternitie shall trample on deathes pate,
And Iustice shall surcease when all be iust:
Thus time, beleefe, death, justice, shall surcease,
By date, assurance, eternity, and peace.

Thus breathing from the Center of his soule,
The tragick accents of his extasie,
His sun-set eyes gan here and there to roule,
Like one surprisde with sodaine lunacie:
And being rouzde out of melancholly,
Flye whirle-winde thoughts vnto the heauens quoth he.

Now in the Ocean Tytan quencht his flame,
And summond Cinthya to set up her light,
The heauens with their glorious starry frame,
Preparde to crowne the sable-vayled night:
When Rowland from this time consumed stock,
With stone-colde hart now stalketh towards his flock.

Quid queror? & toto facio conuicia coelo:
Di quo{que} habent oculos, di quo{que} pectus habent.

THE SECOND EGLOG.

Wynken of mans frayle wayning age
declares the simple truth,

And doth by Rowlands harmes reprooue
Mottos vnbrideled youth.

Motto
MIght my youths mirth delight thy aged yeeres,
My gentle shepheard father of vs all,
Wherewith I why lome Joy'd my lovely feeres,
Chanting sweete straines of heauenly pastorall.

Now would I tune my miskins on this Greene,
And frame my muse those vertues to vnfold,
Of that sole Phenix Bird, my lives sole Queene:
Whose locks done staine, the three times burnisht gold.

But melancholie grafted in thy Braine,
My Rimes seeme harsh, to thy vnrelisht taste,
Thy droughthy wits, not long refresht with raigne,
Parched with heat, done wither now and waste.

Wynken
Indeed my Boy, my wits been all forlorne,
My flowers decayd, with winter-withered frost,
My clowdy set eclips'd my cherefull morne,
That Iewell gone wherein I joyed most.

My dreadful thoughts been drawen vpon my face,
In blotted lines with ages iron pen,
The lothlie morpheu saffroned the place,
Where beuties damaske daz'd the eies of men.

A cumber-world, yet in the world am left,
A fruitles plot, with brambles ouergrowne,
Misliued man of my worlds joy bereft,
Hart-breaking cares the ofspring of my mone.

Those daintie straines of my well tuned reed,
Which manie a time haue pleasd my wanton eares,
Nor sweet, nor pleasing thoughts in me done breed,
But tell the follies of my wandring yeares.

Those poysned pils been biding at my hart,
Those loathsome drugs of my youths vanitie,
Sweete seem'd they once, ful bitter now and tart,
Ay me consuming corosiues they be.

Motto
Even so I weene, for thy olde ages feuer,
Deemes sweetest potions bitter as the gall,

And thy colde Pallat hauing lost her sauour,
Receives no comfort in a cordiall.

Wynken
As thou art now, was I a gamesome boy,
Though staru'd with wintred eld as thou do'st see,
And well I know thy swallow-winged joy,
Shalbe forgotten as it is in me.

When on the Arche of thine eclipsed eies,
Time hath ingrau'd deepe characters of death,
And sun-burnt age thy kindlie moisture dries,
Thy wearied lungs be niggards of thy breath,

Thy brawne-falne armes, thy camock-bended backe,
The time-plow d furrowes in thy fairest field,
The Southsaiers of natures wofull wrack,
When blooming age must stoupe to starued eld,

When Lillie white is of a tawnie die,
Thy fragrant crimson turn'd ash-coloured pale,
Thy skin orecast with rough embroderie,
And cares rude pencell, quite disgrac'd thy sale,

When downe-beds heat must thawe thy frozen cold,
And luke-warme brothes recure Phlebotomie,
And when the bell is readie to be tol'd,
To call the wormes to thine Anatomie:
Remember then my boy, what once I said to thee.

Now am I like the knurrie-bulked Oke,
Whome wasting eld hath made a toombe of dust,
Whose windvfallen branches fold by tempest stroke,
His barcke consumes with canker wormed rust

And though thou seemst like to the bragging bryer,
As gay as is the mornings Marygolde,
Yet shortly shall thy sap be drie and seere,
Thy gaudy Blossomes blemished with colde.

Even such a wanton, an vnruly swayne,
was little Rowland, when of yore as he,
Upon the Beechen tree on yonder playne,
Carued this rime of loves Idolatrie.

The Gods delight, the heauens hie spectacle,
Earths greatest glory, worlds rarest miracle.

Fortunes fayr'st mistresse, vertues surest guide,
Loves Gouernesse, and natures chiefest pride.

Delights owne darling, honours cheefe defence,
Chastities choyce, and wisdomes quintessence.

Conceipts sole Riches thoughts only treasure,
Desires true hope, loyes sweetest pleasure.

Mercies due merite, valeurs iust reward,
Times fayrest fruite, fames strongest guarde.

Yea she alone, next that eternall he,
The expresse Image of eternitie.

Motto

Oh divine love, which so aloft canst raise,
And lift the minde out of this earthly mire,
And do'st inspire the pen with so hie prayse,
As with the heauens doth equal mans desire.

Thou lightning flame of sacred Poesie,
Whose furie doth incense the swelling braines,
As drawes to thee by heauen-bred Sympathie,
The sweete delights of highest soaring vaines:

Who doth not helpe to deck thy holy Shrine,
With Mirtle, and triumphant Lawrell tree?
Who will not say that thou art most divine?
Or who doth not confesse thy deitie?

Wynken

A foolish boy, full ill is he repayed,
For now the wanton pines in endles paine,
And sore repents what he before missaide,
So may they be which can so lewdly faine.

Now hath this yonker torne his tressed lockes,
And broke his pipe which sounded erst so sweete,
Forsaking his companions and their flocks,
And casts his gayest garland at his feete.

And being shrowded in a homely cote,
And full of sorrow as a man might be,
He tun'd his Rebeck with a mournfull note,
And thereto sang this dolefull elegie.

Tell me fayre flocke (if so you can conceaue)

The sodaine cause of my night-sunnes eclipse,
If this be wrought me my light to bereaue,
By Magick spels, from some inchanting lips
Or vgly Saturne from his combust sent,
This fat all presage of deaths dreryment.

Oh cleerest day-starre, honored of mine eyes,
Yet sdaynst mine eyes should gaze upon thy light,
Bright morning sunne, who with thy sweet arise,
Expell'st the clouds of my harts lowring might,
Goddes reiecting sweetest sacrifice,
Of mine eyes teares ay offered to thine eyes.

May purest heauens scorne my soules pure desires?
Or holy shrines hate Pilgrims orizons?
May sacred temples gaynsay sacred prayers?
Or Saints refuse the poores deuotions?
Then Orphane thoughts with sorrow be you waind,
When loves Religion shalbe thus prophayn'd.

Yet needes the earth must droupe with visage sad;
When silver dewes been turn'd to bitter stormes,
The Cheerefull Welkin once in sables clad,
Her frownes foretell poore humaine creatures harmes.
And yet for all to make amends for this,
The clouds sheed teares and weepen at my misse.

Motto
Woe's me for him that pineth so in payne,
Alas poore Rowland, how it pities me,
So faire a baite should breed so foule a bayne,
Or humble shewes should couer crueltie.

Winken
Beware by him thou foolish wanton swayne,
By others harmes thus maist thou learne to heede,
Beautie and wealth been fraught with hie disdaine,
Beleeue it as a Maxim of thy Creede.

Motto
If that there be such woes and paines in love,
Woe be to him that list the same to proue.

Wynken
Yes thou shalt find, if thou desir'st to proue,
There is no hell, vnto the paines in love.

Rowland and Perkin both Ifeere, in field upon a day,
With little Robin redbrests Round, doe passe the time away.

Perkin
Rowland for shame awake thy drowsie muse,
Time plaies the hunts-up to thy sleepie head,
Why li'st thou here as thou hadst long been dead, foule idle swayne?

Who euer heard thy pipe and pleasing vaine,
And doth but heare this scurrill minstralcy.
These noninos of filthie ribauldry, that doth not muse.

Then slumber not with foule Endymion,
But tune thy reede to dapper virelayes,
And sing a while of blessed Betas prayse, faire Beta she:

In thy sweete song so blessed may'st thou bee,
For learned Collin laies his pipes to gage,
And is to fayrie gone a Pilgrimage: the more our mone.

Rowland
What Beta? shepheard, she is Pans belou'd,
Faire Betas praise beyond our straine doth stretch,
Her notes too hie for my poore pipe to reach, poore oten reede:

So farre vnfit to speake of worthies deede,
But set my stops vnto a lower kay,
Whereas a horne-pipe I may safelie play, yet vnreprooʋ'd.

With flatterie my muse could never fage,
Nor could affect such vaine scurrility,
To please lewd Lorrels, in their foolery, too base and vile:

Nor but a note yet will I raise my stile,
My selfe aboue Will Piper to aduance,
Which so bestirs him at the morris dance, for pennie wage.

Perkin
Rowland, so toyes oft times esteemed are,
And fashions euer changing with the time,
Then frolick it a while in lustie rime, with mirth and glee:

And let me heare that Roundelay of thee,
Which once thou sangst to me in laneueer.
When Robin-redbrest sitting on a breere, the burthen bare.

Rowland
Well needes I must yet with a heauie hart:
But were not Beta sure I would not sing,
Whose praise the ecchoes never cease to ring, vnto the skies.

Pirken
Be blith good Rowland then, and cleere thine eyes:
And now sith Robin to his roost is gone,
Good Rowland then supplie the place alone, and shew thy arte.

O thou fayre silver Thames: ô cleerest chrystall flood,
Beta alone the Phenix is, of all thy watery brood,
The Queene of Uirgins onely she:
And thou the Queene of floods shalt be:
Let all thy Nymphes be joyfull then to see this happy day,
Thy Beta now alone shalbe the subiect of my laye.

With daintie and delight some straines of sweetest virelayes:
Come lovely shepheards sit we down & chant our Betas prayse:
And let us sing: so rare a verse,
Our Betas prayses to reheaerse
That little Birds shall silent be, to heare poore shepheards sing,
And riuers backward bend their course, & flow vnto the spring.

Range all thy swannes faire Thames together on a rancke,
And place them duely one by one, upon thy stately banck,
Then set together all a good,
Recording to the silver stood,
And craue the tunefull Nightingale to helpe you with her lay,
The Osel & the Throstlecocke, chiefe musick of our maye.

O see what troups of Nimphs been sporting on the strands,
And they been blessed Nimphs of peace, with Oliues in their
How meryly the Muses sing, (hands.
That all the flowry Medowesring,
And Beta sits upon the banck, in purple and in pall,
And she the Queene of Muses is, and weares the Corinall.

Trim up her Golden tresses with Apollos sacred tree,
ô happy sight vnto all those that love and honor thee,
The Blessed Angels haue prepar'd,
A glorious Crowne for thy reward,
Not such a golden Crowne as haughtie Caesar weares,
But such a glittering starry Crowne as Ariadne beares.

Make her a goodly Chapilet of azur'd Colombine,
And wreath about her Coronet with sweetest Eglentine:

Bedeck our Beta all with Lillies,
And the dayntie Daffadillies,
With Roses damask, white, and red, and fairest flower delice,
With Cowslips of Jerusalem, and cloves of Paradice.

O thou fayre torch of heauen, the dayes most deerest light,
And thou bright-shyning Cinthya, the glory of the night:
You starres the eyes of heauen,
And thou the glyding leuen,
And thou ô gorgeous Iris with all strange Colours dyed,
When she streams foorth her rayes, then dasht is all your pride.

See how the day stands still, admiring of her face,
And time loe stretcheth foorth her armes, thy Beta to imbrace,
The Syrens sing sweete layes,
The Trytons sound her prayse,
Goe passe on Thames and hie thee fast vnto the Ocean sea,
And let thy billowes there proclaime thy Betas holy-day.

And water thou the blessed roote of that greene Oliue tree,
With whose sweete shadow, al thy bancks with peace preserued
Lawrell for Poets and Conquerours, (be,
And mirtle for Loues Paramours:
That fame may be thy fruit, the boughes preseru'd by peace,
And let the mournfist Cipres die, now stormes & tempests cease.

Wee'l straw the shore with pearle where Beta walks alone,
And we wil paue her princely Bower with richest Indian stone,
Perfume the ayre and make it sweete,
For such a Goddesse it is meete,
For if her eyes for purity contend with Tytans light,
No maruaile then although they so doe dazell humaine sight.

Sound out your trumpets then, from Londons stately towres,
To beat the stormie windes a back & calme the raging showres,
Set too the Cornet and the flute,
The Orpharyon and the Lute,
And tune the Taber and the pipe, to the sweet violons,
And moue the thunder in the ayre, with lowdest Clarions.

Beta long may thine Altars smoke, with yeerely sacrifice,
And long thy sacred Temples may their Saboths solemnize,
Thy shepheards watch by day and night,
Thy Mayds attend the holy light,
And thy large empyre stretch her armes from east vnto the west,
And thou vnder thy feet mayst tread, that soule seuen-headed beast.

Perken

Thanks gentle Rowland for my Roundelay,
And bless'd be Beta burthen of thy song,
The shepheards Goddesse may she florish long, ô happie she.

Her yeares and dayes thrice doubled may they bee.
Triumphing Albion clap thy hands for joy,
And pray the heauens may shield her from anoy, so will I pray.

Rowland
So doe, ānd when my milk-white eawes haue yeande,
Beta shall haue the firstling of the foulde,
I le burnish all his hornes with finest gould, and paynt his fleece with purple grayne.

Perkin
Beleeue me as I am true shepheards swayne,
Then for thy love all other I forsake,
And vnto thee my selfe I will betake, with fayth vnfayn'd.

Ipse ego thura dabo, fumosis candidus aris:
Ipse feram ante tuos munera vota pedes.

THE FOURTH EGLOG.

Wynken be wayleth Elphinslosse,
the God of Poesie,
with Rowlands rime ecleepd the tears
of the greene Hawthorne tree.

Gorbo.
Well met good wynken, whither doest thou wend?
How hast thou far'd sweet shepherd many a yeer?
May wynken thus his daies in darkenes spend?
Who I haue knowne for piping had no peere?

Where been those fayre flocks thou wert wont to guide?
What? been they dead? or hap'd on some mischance,
Or mischiefe hath their master else betide,
Or Lordly Love hath cast thee in a trance.

What man? lets still be merie whilst we may,
And take a truce with sorrow for a time,
And let us passe this wearie winters day,
In reading Riddles, or in making rime.

Wynken
Ah woe's me Gorbo, mirth is farre away,

Mirth may not soiourne with black malcontent,
The lowring aspect of this dismall day,
The winter of my sorrow doth augment.

My song is now a swanne-like dying song,
And my conceipts, the deepe conceipts of death,
My heart becom'n a very hell of wrong,
My breast the irksome prison of my breath.

I loth my life, I loth the dearest light,
Com'n is my night, when once appeeres the day,
The blessed sunne seemes odious in my sight,
No song may like me but the shreech-owles lay.

Gorbo
What mayst thou be, that old wynkin de word,
Whose thred-bare wits o'rworne with melancholly,
Once so delightsome at the shepheards boord,
But now forlorne with thy selues self-wild folly.

I think thou dot'st in thy gray-bearded age,
Or brusd with sinne, for thy youths sin art sory,
And vow'st for thy? a solemne pilgrimage,
To holy Hayles or Patricks Purgatory.

Come sit we downe vnder this Hawthorne tree.
The morrowes light shall lend us daie enough,
And tell a tale of Gawen or Sir Guy,
Of Robin Hood, or of good Clema Clough.

Or else some Romant vnto us areed,
Which good olde Godfrey taught thee in thy youth,
Of noble Lords and Ladies gentle deede,
Or of thy love, or of thy lasses truth.

Winken
Gorbo, my Comfort is accloyd with care,
A new mishap my wonted joyes hath crost:
Then meruaile not although my musicke iarre,
When she the Author of her mirth hath lost,

Elphin is dead, and in his graue is laid,
Our lives delight whilst lovely Elphin liued,
What cruell fate hath so the time berraid,
The widow world of all her joyes depriued.

O cursed death, Lives fearsull enemie,
Times poysned sickle: Tyrants revenging pride:

Thou blood-sucker, Thou childe of infamie:
Deuouring Tiger: slaughtering homicide:
Ill hast thou done, and ill may thee betide.

Naught hast thou got, the earth hath wonne the most,
Nature is payd the interest of her due,
Pan hath receau'd, what him so dearly cost,
O heauens his vertues doe belong to you.

A heauenly clowded in a humaine shape,
Rare substance, in so rough a barcke Iclad,
Of Pastorall, the liuely springing sappe,
Though mortall thou, thy fame immortall made.

Spel-charming Prophet, sooth-divining seer,
ô heauenly musicke of the highest spheare,
Sweet sounding trump, soule-rauishing desire,
Thou stealer of mans heart, inchanter of the eare.

God of Inuention, loues deere Mercury,
Joy of our Lawrell, pride of all our joy:
The essence of all Poets divinitie,
Spirit of Orpheus: Pallas lovely boy.

But all my words shalbe dissolu'd to teares,
And my tears fountaines shall to riuers grow:
These Riuers to the floods of my dispaires,
And these shall make an Ocean of my woe.

His rare desarts, shall kindle my desire,
With burning zeale, the brands of mine vnrest,
My sighes in adding sulphure to this fire,
Shall frame another AEtna in my breast.

Planets reserue your playnts till dismall day,
The ruthles rockes but newly haue begonne,
And when in drops they be dissolu'd away,
Let heauens begin to weepe when earth hath done.

Then tune thy pipe and I will sing alaye,
Upon his death by Rowland of the rocke,
Sitting with me this other stormy day,
In you sayre field attending on our flock.

Gorbo
This shall content me Wynken wondrous well,
And in this mistie wether keepe us waking,
To heare ofhim, who whylome did excell,

In such a song of learned Rowlands making.

Melpomine put on thy mourning Gaberdine,
And set thy song vnto the dolefull Base,
And with thy sable vayle shadow thy face,
With weeping verse,
Attend his hearse,
Whose blessed soule the heauens doe now enshrine.

Come Nymphs and with your Rebecks ring his knell,
Warble forth your wamenting harmony,
And at his drery fat all obsequie,
With Cypres bowes,
Maske your fayre Browes,
And beat your breasts to chyme his burying peale.

Thy birth-day was to all our joye, the even,
And on thy death this dolefull song we sing,
Sweet Child of Pan, and the Castalian spring,
Unto our endles mone,
From us why art thou gone,
To fill up that sweete Angels quier in heauen.

O whylome thou thy lasses dearest love,
When with greene Lawrell she hath crowned thee,
Immortall mirror of all Poesie:
The Muses treasure,
The Graces pleasure,
Reigning with Angels now in heauen aboue.

Our mirth is now depriu'd of all her glory,
Our Taburins in dolefull dumps are drownd.
Our viols want their sweet and pleasing sound,
Our melodie is mar'd
And we of joyes debard,
Oh wicked world so mutable and transitory.

O dismall day, bereauer of delight,
O stormy winter sourse of all our sorrow,
ô most vntimely and eclipsed morrow,
To rob us quite
Of all delight,
Darkening that starre which euer shone so bright:

Oh Elphin, Elphin, Though thou hence be gone,
In spight of death yet shalt thou liue for aye,
Thy Poesie is garlanded with Baye:
And still shall blaze

Thy lasting prayse:
Whose losse poore shepherds euer shall bemone.

Come Girles, and with Carnations decke his graue,
With damaske Roses and the hyacynt:
Come with sweete Williams, Marioram and Mynt,
With precious Balmes,
With hymnes and psalmes,
His funerall deserues no lesse at all to haue.

But see where Elphin sits in fayre Elizia,
Feeding his flocke on yonder heauenly playne,
Come and behold, yon lovely shepheards swayne,
Piping his fill,
On yonder hill,
Tasting sweete Nectar, and Ambrosia.

Gorbo
Oh how thy plaints (sweete friend) renew my payne,
In listning thus to thy lamenting cries:
That from the tempest of my troubled brayne,
See how the floods been risen in mine eyes.

And being now a full tide of our teares,
It is full time to stop the streame of griefe,
Lest drowning in the floods of our despaires,
We want our lives, wanting our soules reliefe.

But now the sunne beginneth to decline,
And whilest our woes been in repeating here,
Yon little eluish moping Lamb of mine,
Is all betangled in yon crawling Brier.

Optima prima ferè manibus rapiuntur auaris:
Implentur numer is deteriora suis.

THE FIFTH EGLOG.

This lustie swayne bis lowly quill, to higher notes doth rayse,
And in Ideas person paynts, his lovely lasses prayse.

Motto
Come frolick it a while my lustie swayne,
Let's see if time haue yet reuiu'd in thee,
Or if there be remayning but a grayne,
Of the olde stocke of famous poesie,

Or but one slip yet left of this same sacred tree.

Or if reseru'd from elds deuouring rage,
Recordes of vertue, Aye memoriall,
Left to the world as learnings lasting gage,
Or if the prayse of worthy pastorall,
May tempt thee now, or mooue thee once at all.

To Fortunes Orphanes Nature hath bequeath'd,
That mighty Monarchs seldome haue possest,
From highest Heauen, this influence is breath'd,
A most divine impression in the breast, (feast.
And those whom Fortune pines doth Nature often

Ti's not the troupes of paynted Imagerie,
Nor these worlds Idols, our worlds Idiots gazes,
Our forgers of suppos'd Gentillitie,
When he his great, great Grand-sires glory blases,
And paints out fictions in base coyned Phrases.

For honour naught regards, nor followeth fame,
These silken pictures shewed in euery streete:
Of Idlenes comes euill, of pride ensueth shame,
And blacke obliuion is their winding sheete,
And all their glory troden vnder feete.

Though Enuie sute her seven-times poysned dartes,
Yet purest golde is seven times try'd in fier,
True valeur lodgeth in the lowlest harts,
Vertue is in the minde, not in th'attyre,
Nor stares at starres; nor stoups at filthy myre.

Rowland
I may not sing of such as fall, nor clyme,
Nor chaunt of armes, nor of heroique deedes,
It fitteth not poore shepheards rurall rime,
Nor is agreeing with my oaten reedes,
Nor from my quill, grosse flatterie proceedes.

Vnsitting tearmes, nor false dissembling smiles,
Shall in my lines, nor in my stile appeare,
Worlds fawning fraud, nor like deceitfull guiles,
No, no, my muse none such shall soiourne here,
Nor any bragges of hope nor signes of base despaire,

No fatall dreades nor fruitles vaine desires,
Nor caps, nor curtsies to a paynted wall,
Nor heaping rotten sticks on needles fires,

Ambitious thoughts to clime nor fearcs to fall,
A minde voyd of mistrust, and free from seruile thral.

Foule slander thou suspitions Bastard Child,
Selfe-eating Impe from vipers poysned wombe,
Foule swelling to ade with lothly spots defil'd,
Vile Aspis bred within the ruinde tombe,
Eternall death for euer be thy doombe.

Still be thou shrouded in blacke pitchie night,
Luld with the horror of night-rauens song,
Let foggie mistes, clowd and eclipse thy light,
Thy wooluish teeth chew out thy venomd tongue,
With Snakes and adders be thy body stong.

Motto
Nor these, nor these, may like thy lowlie quill,
As of too hie, or of too base a straine,
Vnfitting thee, and sdeyned ofthy skill,
Nor yet according with a shepheards vayne,
Nor no such subiect may beseeme a swayne.

Then tune thy reede vnto Ideas prayse:
And teach the woods to wonder at her name:
Thy lowlie notes here mayst thou learne to rayse,
And make the ecchoes blazen out her name,
The lasting trumpe of Phebes lasting fame.

Thy Temples then shall with greene bayes be dight,
Thy Egle-soring muse upon her wing,
With her fayre silver wings shall take her flight,
To that hie welked tower where Angels sing,
From thence to fetch the tutch of her sweete string.

Rowland
Oh hie inthronized loue, in thy Olympicke raigne,
Oh battel-waging Marte, oh sage-saw'd Mercury,
Oh Golden shrined Sol, Uenus loves soueraigne,
Oh dreadfull Saturne, flaming aye with furie,
Moyst-humord Cinthya, Author of Lunacie,
Conjoyne helpe to erect our faire Ideas trophie.

Oh Tresses of faire Phoebus stremed die,
Oh blessed load-starre lending purest light,
Oh Paradice of heauenly tapistrie,
Angels sweete musick, ô my soules delight,
O fayrest Phebe passing euery other light.

Whose presence joyes the earths decayed state,
Whose counsels are registred in the sphere,
Whose sweete reflecting clearenes doth amate,
The starrie lights, and makes the Sunne more fayre,
Whose breathing sweete perfumeth all the ayre.

Thy snowish necke, fayre Natures tresurie,
Thy swannish breast, the hauen of lasting blisse,
Thy cheekes the bancks of Beauties usurie,
Thy heart the myne, where goodnes gotten is,
Thy lips those lips which Cupid joyes to kisse.

And those fayre hands within whose lovely palmes,
Fortune divineth happie Augurie,
Those straightest fingers dealing heauenly almes,
Pointed with pur'st of Natures Alcumie,
Where love sits looking in loves palmistrie.

And those fayre Ivorie columnes which upreare,
That Temple built by heauens Geometrie,
And holiest Flamynes sacrifizen theare,
Vnto that heauenly Queene of Chastitie,
Where vertues burning lamps can never quenched be.

Thence see the fairest light that euer shone,
That cleare which doth worlds cleerenes quite sur|passe,
Braue Phoebus chayred in his golden throane,
Beholding him, in this pure Christall glasse,
See here the fayrest fayre that euer was.

Delicious fountaine, liquid christalline,
Mornings vermilion, verdant spring-times pride,
Purest of purest, most refined fine,
With crimson tincture curiously Idy'd,
Mother of Muses, great Apollos bride.

Earths heauen, worlds wonder, hiest house of fame,
Reuiuer of the dead, eye-killer of the liue,
Belou'd of Angels, Vertues greatest name,
Fauors rar'st feature, beauties prospectiue,
Oh that my verse thy vertues could contriue.

That stately Theater on whose fayre stage,
Each morall vertue actes a princely part,
Where euery scene pronounced by a Sage,
Eternizeth divinest Poets Arte,
Joyes the beholders eyes, and glads the hearers hart.

The worlds memorials, that sententious booke,
Where euery Comma, points a curious phrase,
Upon whose method, Angels joye to looke:
At euery Colon, Wisdomes selfe doth pause,
And euery Period hath his hie applause.

Read in her eyes a Romant of delights,
Read in her words the prouerbs of the wise,
Read in her life the holy vestall rites,
Which love and vertue sweetly moralize:
And she the Academ of vertues exercise.

But on thy volumes who is there may comment,
When as thy selfe hath Arts selfe vndermined:
Or vndertake to coate thy learned margent,
When learnings lines are euer enterlined,
And purest words, are in thy mouth refined.

Knewest thou thy vertues, oh thou fayr'st of fayrest,
Thou earths sole Phenix, of the world admired,
Vertue in thee repurify'd and rarest,
Whose endles fame by time is not expired,
Then of thy selfe would thy selfe be admired.

But arte wants arte to frame so pure a Myrror,
Where humaine eyes may view thy vertues beautie,
When fame is so surprised with the terror,
wanting to pay the tribute of her duetie,
with colours who can paint out vertues beautie.

But since vnperfect are the perfects colours,
And skill is so vnskilfull how to blaze thee:
Now will I make a myrror of my dolours,
And in my teares then looke thy selfe and prayse thee,
Oh happy I, if such a glasse might please thee.

Goe gentle windes and whisper in her eare,
and tell Idea how much I adore her,
And thou my flock, reporte vnto my fayre,
How she excelleth all that went before her,
Tell her the very foules in ayre adore her.

And thou cleare Brooke by whose fayre silver streame,
Grow those tall Okes where I haue caru'd her name,
Conuay her praise to Neptunes watery Realme,
Refresh the rootes of her still growing fame,
And teach the Dolphins to resound her name.

Motto

Cease shepheard cease, reserue thy Muses store,
Till after time shall teach thy Oaten reede,
Aloft in ayre with Egles wings to sore,
And sing in honor of some worthies deede,
To serue Idea in some better steede.

She sees not shepheard, no she will not see,
her rarest vertues blazond by thy quill,
Nor knowes the effect the same hath wrought in thee,
The very tuch and anuile of thy skill,
And this is that which bodeth all thy ill.

Yet if her vertues glorie shall decay,
Or if her beauties flower shall hap to fall,
Or any cloud eclipse her sun-shine day,
Then looke (Idea) in thy pastorall,
And thou thy vertues vnto minde shalt call,

Rowland

Shepheard farewell, the skies begin to lowre,
Yon pitchie clowd which hangeth in the West,
I feare me doth presage some sodaine showre,
Come let us home, for so I think it best,
For all our flocks been laid them downe to rest.

Motto

And if thou list to come vnto my Coate,
Although (God knowes) my cheere be to too small,
And wealth with me was never yet afloate,
Yet take in gree what euer doe befall,
And wee will sit, and sing a mery madrigall.

Rowland

Per superos iuro testes, pampamque Deorum,
Te Dominam nobis tempus in omne fore.

Motto

Nos quoque per totum pariter cantabimur orbem,
Iunctáque semper erunt nomina nostratuis.

THE SIXTH EGLOG.

Good Gorbo cals to mind the fame,
Of our old Ancestrie:
And Perkin sings Pandoras prayse,

The Muse of Britanye.

Perkin
All haile good Gorbo, yet return'd at last,
What tell me man? how goes the world with thee?
What is it worse then it was wont to be?
Or been thy youthfull dayes already past?
Haue patience man, for wealth will come and goe,
And to the end the world shall ebbe and flowe.

The valiant man, whose thoughts on hie been placed,
And sees sometime how fortune list to rage,
With wisdome still his actions so doth gage,
As with her frownes he no whit is disgraced,
And when she fawnes, and turnes her squinting eye,
Bethinks him then, of her inconstancie.

When as the Cullian, and the viler Clowne,
Who with the swine, on draffe sets his desire,
And thinks no life to wallowing in the myre,
In stormie tempest, dying layes him downe,
Yet tasting weale, the asse begins to bray,
And feeling woe, the beast consumes away.

Gorbo
So said the Sage in his Philofophie,
The Lordly hart inspir'd with noblesse,
With courage doth his crosses still suppresse,
His patience doth his passions mortifie,
When other folke this paine cannot endure,
Because they want this med'cine for their cure.

Perkin
And yet oft times the world I doe admire,
When as the wise and vertuous men I see,
Be hard beset with neede and pouertie,
And lewdest fooles to highest things aspire,
What should I say? that fortune is to blame?
Or vnto whome should I impute this shame.

Gorbo
Vertue and Fortune never could agree,
Foule Fortune euer was faire vertues foe,
Blinde Fortune blindly doth her gifts bestowe,
But vertue wise, and wisely doth foresee,
They tall which trust to fortunes fickle wheele,
But staied by vertue, men shall never reele.

Perkin

If so, why should she not be more regarded,
Why should men cherish vice and villanie,
And maintaine sinne and basest rogerie,
And vertue thus so slightly be rewarded,
This shewes that we full deepe dissemblers be,
And all we doe, but meere hypocrisie.

Gorbo

Where been those Nobles, Perkin, where been they?
Where been those worthies, Perkin, which of yore,
This gentle Ladie did so much adore?
And for her Impes did with such care puruey,
they been yswadled in their winding sheete,
and she (I thinke) is buried at their feete.

Oh worthy world, wherein those worthies liued,
Unworthy world, of such men so vnworthy,
Unworthy age, of all the most vnworthy,
Which art of these so worthy men depriued,
And inwardly in us is nothing lesse,
Than outwardly that, which we most professe.

Perkin

Nay stay good Gorbo, Vertue is not dead,
Nor all her friends be gone which wonned here,
She lives with one who euer held her deere,
And to her lappe for succour she is fled,
In her sweete bosome, she hath built her nest,
And from the world, even there she lives at rest.

Unto this sacred Ladie she was left,
(To be an heire-loome) by her ancestrie,
And so bequeathed by their legacie,
When on their death-bed, life was them berest:
And as on earth together they remayne,
Together so in heauen they both shall raigne.

Oh thou Pandora, through the world renoun'd,
The glorious light, and load starre of our West,
With all the vertues of the heauens possest,
With mighty groues of holy Lawrell cround,
Erecting learnings long decayed fame,
Heryed and hallowed be thy sacred name.

The flood of Helicon, forspent and drie,
Her sourse decayd with foule obliuion,
The fountaine flowes againe in thee alone,

Where Muses now their thirst may satisfie,
And old Apollo, from Pernassus hill,
May in this spring refresh his droughty quill.

The Graces twisting garlands for thy head,
Thy Iuorie temples deckt with rarest flowers,
Their rootes refreshed with divinest showers,
Thy browes with mirtle all inueloped,
Shepheards erecting trophies to thy praise,
Lauding thy name in songs and heauenly laies.

Sapphos sweete vaine in thy rare quill is seene,
Minerua was a figure of thy worth,
Mnemosine, who brought the Muses forth,
Wonder of Britaine, learnings famous Queene,
Apollo was thy Syer, Pallas her selfe thy mother,
Pandora thou, our Phoebus was thy brother.

Delicious Larke, sweete musick of the morrow,
Cleere bell of Rhetoricke, ringing peales of love,
Joy of the Angels, sent us from aboue,
Enchanting Syren, charmer of all sorrow,
the loftie subiect a heauenly tale,
Thames fairest Swanne, our summers Nightingale.

Arabian Phenix, wonder of thy sexe,
Lovely, chaste, holy, Myracle admired,
With spirit from the highest heauen inspired,
Oh thou alone, whome fame alone respects,
Natures chiefe glory, learnings richest prize,
Hie Ioues Empresa, vertues Paradize.

Oh glorie of thy nation, beauty of thy name,
Joy of thy countrey, blesser of thy birth,
Thou blazing Comet, Angel of the earth,
Oh Poets Goddesse, sun-beame of their fame:
whome time through many worlds hath sought to
thou peerles Paragon of woman kinde. (find,

Thy glorious Image, gilded with the sunne,
Thy lockes adorn'd with an immortall crowne,
Mounted aloft, upon a Chrystal throne,
When by thy death, thy life shalbe begun:
The blessed Angels tuning to the spheares,
With Gods sweete musick, charme thy sacred eares.

From Fayrie Ile, deuided from the mayne,
To vtmost Thuly fame transports thy name,

To Garamant shall thence conuey the same,
Where taking wing, and mounting up againe,
From parched banckes on sun-burnt. Affricks shore,
Shall flie as farre as erst she came of yore.

And gentle Zephire from his pleasant bower,
Whistling sweete musick to the shepheards rime,
The Ocean billowes duely keeping time,
Playing upon Neptunus brazen tower:
Lovers of learning shouting out their cries,
Shaking the Center with th'applaudities.

Whilst that great engine, on her axeltree,
Doth role about the vaultie circled Globe,
Whilst morning mantleth, in her purple Robe,
Or Tytan poste his sea Queenes bower to see,
whilst Phoebus crowne, adornes the starrie skie,
Pandoras fame so long shall never die.

When all our silver swans shall cease to sing,
And when our groues shall want their Nightingales,
When hils shall heare no more our shepheards tales,
Nor ecchoes with our Roundelayes shall ring,
the little birdes long listning to thy fame,
shall teach their ofspring to record thy name.

Ages shall tell such wonders of thy name,
And thou in death thy due desert shalt haue,
That thou shalt be immortall in thy graue,
Thy vertues adding force vnto thy fame,
So that vertue with thy fames wings shall flie,
And by thy fame shall vertue never die.

Upon thy toombe shall spring a Lawrell tree,
Whose sacred shade shall serue thee for an hearse,
Upon whose leaues (in golde) ingrau'd this verse,
Dying she lives, whose like shall never be,
A spring of Nectar flowing from this tree,
The fountayne of eternali memorie.

To adorne the trrumph of eternitie,
Drawne with the steedes which dragge the golden sunne,
Thy wagon through the milken way shall runne,
Millions of Angels still attending thee,
Millions of Saints shall thy lives prayses sing,
Pend with the quill of an Archangels wing.

Gorbo

Long may Pandora weare the Lawrell crowne,
The ancient glory of her noble Peers,
And as the Egle: Lord renew her yeeres,
Long to upholde the proppe of our renowne,
Long may she be as she hath euer beene,
The lowly handmaide of the Fayrie Queene.

Non mihi mille placent: non sum desertor Amoris:
Tu mihi (si quafides) curaperennis eris.

THE SEVENTH EGLOG.

Borrill an aged shepheard swaine, with reasons doth reprooue,
Batte a foolish want on boy, but lately falne in love.

Batte
Borill, why sit'st thou musing in thy coate?
like dreaming Merlyn in his drowsie Cell,
What may it be with learning thou doest doate,
or art inchanted with some Magick spell?
Or wilt thou an Hermites life professe?
And bid thy beades heare like an Ancoresse?

See how faire Flora decks our fields with flowers,
and clothes our groues in gaudie summers greene,
And wanton Uer distils rose-water showers,
to welcome Ceres, haruests hallowed Queene,
Who layes abroad her lovely sun-shine haires,
Crown'd with great garlands of her golden eares.

Now shepheards layne their blankets all awaie,
and in their lackets minsen on the plaines,
And at the riuers fishen daie by daie,
now none so frolicke as the shepheards swaines,
Why liest thou here then in thy loathsome caue,
As though a man were buried quicke in graue.

Borrill
Batte, my coate from tempest standeth free,
when stately towers been often shakt with wind,
And wilt thou Batte, come and sit with me?
contented life here shalt thou onely finde,
Here mai'st thou caroll Hymnes, and sacred Psalmes,
And hery Pan, with orizons and almes.

And scorne the crowde of such as cogge for pence,

and waste their wealth in sinfull brauerie,
Whose gaine is losse, whose thrift is lewd expence,
and liuen still in golden slauery:
Wondring at toyes, as foolish worldlings doone,
Like to the dogge which barked at the moone.

Here maist thou range the goodly pleasant field,
And search out simples to procure thy heale,
What sundry vertues hearbs and flowres doe yeeld,
Gainst griefe which may thy sheepe or thee assaile:
Here mayst thou hunt the little harmeles Hare,
Or else entrap false Raynard in a snare.

Or if thou wilt in antique Romants reede,
Of gentle Lords and ladies that of yore,
In forraine lands atchieu'd their noble deede,
And been renownd from East to Westerne shore:
Or learne the shepheards nice astrolobie,
To know the Planets moouing in the skie.

Batte
Shepheard these things been all too coy for mee,
Whose lustie dayes should still be spent in mirth,
These mister artes been better fitting thee, (earth:
Whose drouping dayes are drawing towards the
What thinkest thou? my iolly peacocks trayne,
Shall be acoyd and brooke so foule a stayne?

These been for such as make them votarie,
And take them to the mantle and the ring,
And spenden day and night in dotarie,
Hammering their heads, musing on heauenly thing,
And whisper still of sorrow in their bed,
And done despise all love and lustie head:

Like to the curre, with anger well neere woode,
who makes his kennel in the Oxes stall,
And snarleth when he seeth him take his foode,
and yet his chaps can chew no hay at all.
Borrill, even so it fareth now with thee,
And with these wisards of thy mysterie.

Borrill
Sharpe is the thorne, full soone I see by thee,
bitter the blossome, when the fruite is sower,
And early crook d, that will a Camock bee,
Rough is the winde before a sodayne shower:
Pittie thy wit should be so wrong mislead,

And thus be guyded by a giddie head.

Ah foolish else, I inly pittie thee,
misgouerned by thy lewd brainsick will:
The hidden baytes, ah fond thou do'st not see,
nor find'st the cause which breedeth all thy ill:
Thou think'st all golde, that hath a golden shew,
And art deceiu'd, for it is nothing soe.

Such one art thou as is the little flie,
who is so crowse and gamesome with the flame,
Till with her busines and her nicetie,
her nimble wings are scorched with the same,
Then fals she downe with pitteous buzzing note,
And in the fier doth sindge her mourning cote.

Batte
Alas good man I see thou ginst to raue,
thy wits done erre, and misse the cushen quite,
Because thy head is gray and wordes been graue,
Thou think'st thereby to draw me from delight:
What I am young, a goodly Batcheler,
And must liue like the lustie limmeter.

Thy legges been crook'd, thy knees done bend for age,
and I am swift and nimble as the Roe,
Thou art ycouped like a bird in cage,
and in the field I wander too and froe,
Thou must doe penance for thy olde misdeedes,
And make amends, with Auies and with creedes.

For all that thou canst say, I will not let,
for why my fancie strayneth me so sore,
That day and night, my minde is wholy set
on iollie. Love, and iollie Paramore:
Only on love I set my whole delight,
The summers day, and all the winters night.

That pretie Cupid, little god of love,
whose imped wings with speckled plumes been dight,
Who striketh men below, and Gods aboue,
Rouing at randon with his feathered flight,
When lovely Uenus sits and giues the ayme,
And smiles to see her little Bantlings game.

Upon my staffe his statue will I carue,
his bowe and quiuer on his winged backe,
His forked heads, for such as them deserue,

and not of his, an implement shall lacke,
And Uenus in her Litter all of love,
Drawne with a Swanne, a Sparrow, and a Doue.

And vnder him Thesby of Babylon,
and Clcopatra somtime of renowne:
Phillis that died for love of Demophôon,
Then lovely Dido Queen of Carthage towne,
Which euer held god Cupids lawes so deare,
And been canoniz'd in Loves Calendere.

Borrill
Ah wilfull boy, thy follie now I finde,
and hard it is a fooles talke to endure,
Thou art as deafe even as thy god is blinde,
sike as the Saint, sike is the seruiture:
But wilt thou heare a good olde Minstrels song,
A medicine for such as been with love ystong.

Batte
Borrill, sing on I pray thee let us heare,
that I may laugh to see thee shake thy beard,
But take heede Borrill that thy voyce be cleare,
or by my hood thou'lt make us all afeard,
Or els I doubt that thou wilt fright our flockes,
When they shall heare thee barke so like a foxe.

Borrill
Oh spight full way ward wretched love,
Woe to Venus which did nurse thee,
Heauens and earth thy plagues do proue,
Gods and men haue cause to curse thee.
Thoughts griefe, hearts woe,
Hopes paine, bodies languish,
Enutes rage, sleepes foe,
Fancies fraud, soules anguish,
Desires dread, mindes madnes,
Secrets be wrayer, natures error,
Sights deceit, sullens sadnes,
Speeches expence, Cupids terror,

Malcontents melancholly,
Lives slaughter, deaths nurse,
Cares slaue, dotards folly,
Fortunes bayte, worlds curse,
Lookes theft, eyes blindnes,
Selfes will, tongues treason,
Paynes pleasure, wrongs kindnes,

Furies frensie, follies reason:
With cursing thee as I began,
Cursing thee I make an end,
Neither God, neither man,
Neither Fayrie, neither Feend.

Batte

Ah worthy Borrill, here's a goodly song,
now by my belt I never heard a worse:
Olde doting foole, for shame hold thou thy tongue,
I would thy clap were shut up in my purse.
It is thy life, if thou mayst scolde and braule:
Yet in thy words there is no wit at all.

And for that wrong which thou to love hast done,
I will aueng me at this present time,
And in such forte as now thou hast begonne,
I will repeat a carowlet in rime,
Where, Borrill, I vnto thy teeth will proue,
That all my good consisteth in my love.

Borrill

Come on good Batte, I pray thee let us heare?
Much will be sayd, and never a whit the near.

Batte

Love is the heauens fayre aspect, love is the glorie of the earth,
Love only doth our lives direct, love is our guyder from our birth,

Love taught my thoughts at first to flie, love taught mme eyes the way to love,
Love raysed my conceit so hie, love framd my hand his arte to proue.

Love taught my Muse her perfect skill, love gaue me first to Poesies
Love is the Soueraigne of my will, love bound me first to loyalty.

Love was the first that fram'd my speech, love was the first that gaue me grace:
Love is my life and fortunes leech, love made the vertuous giue me place.

Love is the end of my desire, love is the loadstarre of my love,
Love makes my selfe, my selfe admire, love seated my delights aboue.

Love placed honor in my brest, love made me learnings fauoret,
Love made me liked of the best, love first my minde on vertue set.

Love is my life, life is my love, love is my whole felicity,
Love is my sweete, sweete is my love, I am in love, and love in me.

Borrill

Is love in thee? alas poore sillie lad, thou never couldst haue lodg'd a worser guest,
For where he rules no reason can be had, so is he still sworne enemie to rest:
It pitties me to thinke thy springing yeares,
Should still be spent with woes, with sighes, with teares.

Batte
Gramercy Borrill for thy company, for all thy iestes and all thy merrie Bourds,
I still shall long vntill I be with thee, because I find some wisdome in thy words,
But I will watch the next time thou doost ward, (heard.
And sing thee such a lay of love as never shepheard

THE EIGHTH EGLOG.

Good Gorbo of the golden world, and Saturns raigne doth tell,
And afterward doth make reporte, of bonnie Dowsabell.

Motto
Shepheard why creepe we in this lowly vaine,
As though our muse no store at all affordes,
Whilst others vaunt it with the frolicke swayne,
And strut the stage with reperfumed wordes.

See how these yonkers raue it out in rime,
Who make a traffique of their rarest wits,
And in Bellonas buskin tread it fine,
like Bacchus priests raging in franticke fits.

Those mirtle Groues decay'd, done growe againe,
Their rootes refresht with Heliconas spring,
Whose pleasant shade inuites the homely swayne,
To sit him downe and heare the Muses sing.

Then if thy Muse hath spent her wonted zeale,
With Iuie twist thy temples shall be crownd,
Or if she dares hoyse up top-gallant sayle,
Amongst the rest, then may she be renownd.

Gorbe
My boy, these yonkers reachen after fame,
and so done presse into the learned troupe,
With filed quill to glorifie their name,
which otherwise were pend in shamefull coupe.

But this hie obiect hath abiected me,
and I must pipe amongst the lowly sorte,
Those little heard-groomes who admir'd to see,

When I by Moone-shine made the fayries sporte.

Who dares describe the toyles of Hercules,
And puts his hand to fames eternall penne,
Must inuocate the soule of Hercules,
Attended with the troupes of conquered men.

Who writes of thrice renowmed Theseus,
A monster-tamers rare description,
Trophies the iawes of vglie Cerberus,
And paynts out Styx, and fiery Acheron.

My Muse may not affect night-charming spels,
Whose force effects th' Olympicke vault to quake,
Nor call those grysly Goblins from their Cels,
The euer-damned frye of Limbo lake.

And who erects the braue Pyramides,
Of Monarches or renowned warriours,
Neede bath his quill for such attempts as these,
in flowing streames of learned Maros showres.

For when the great worlds conquerer began,
To proue his helmet and his habergeon,
The sweat that from the Poets-God Orpheus ran,
Foretold his Prophets had to play upon.

When Pens and Launces sawe the Olympiad prize,
those chariot triumphes with the Lawrell crowne,
Then gan the worthies glorie first to rise,
And plumes were vayled to the purple gowne.

The grauest Censor, sagest Senator,
With wings of Iustice and Religion,
Mounted the top of Nimrods statelie Tower,
Soring vnto that hie celestiall throne:

Where blessed Angels in their heauenly queares,
Chaunt Anthemes with shrill Syren harmonie,
Tun'd to the sound of those aye-crouding sphears,
Which herien their makers eternitie.

Those who foretell the times of vnborne men,
And future things in foretime augured,
Haue slumbred in that spell-gods darkest den,
Which first inspir'd his prophesiyng head.

Sooth-saying Sibels sleepen long agone,

we haue their reede, but few haue cond their Arte,
Welch-wisard Merlyn, cleueth to a stone,
No Oracle more wonders may impart.

The Infant age could deftly caroll love,
Till greedy thirst of that ambitious honor,
Drew Poets pen, from his sweete lasses glove,
To chaunt of slaughtering broiles & bloody horror.

Then Joues love-theft was priuily discri'd,
How he playd false play in Amphitrios bed,
And how Apollo in the mount of Ide,
Gaue Oenon phisick for her maydenhead.

The tender grasse was then the softest bed,
The pleasant'st shades were deem'd the statelyest hals,
No belly-god with Bacchus banqueted,
Nor paynted ragges then couered rotten wals.

Then simple love with simple vertue way'd,
Flowers the fauours which true fayth reuayled,
Kindnes with kindnes was againe repay'd,
With sweetest kisses couenants were sealed.

Then beauties selfe with her selfe beautified,
scornd payntings pergit, and the borrowed hayre,
Nor monstrous formes deformities did hide,
Nor foule was vernisht with compounded fayre.

The purest fleece then couered purest skin,
For pride as then with Lucifer remaynd:
Deformed fashions now were to begin,
Nor clothes were yet with poysned liquor staynd.

But when the bowels of the earth were sought,
And men her golden intrayles did espie,
This mischiefe then into the world was brought,
This fram'd the mint which coynd our miserie.

Then lofty Pines were by ambition hewne,
And men sea-monsters swamme the brackish flood,
In waynscot tubs, to seeke out worlds vnknowne,
For certain ill to leaue assured good.

The starteling steede is manag'd from the field,
And serues a subiect to the riders lawes,
He whom the churlish bit did never weeld,
Now feels the courb controll his angrie iawes.

The hammering Uulcane spent his wasting fire,
Till he the use of tempred mettals found,
His anuile wrought the steeled cotes attire,
And forged tooles to carue the foe-mans wound.

The Citie builder then intrencht his towres,
And wald his wealth within the fenced towne,
Which afterward in bloudy stormy stours,
kindled that flame which burnt his Bulwarks downe.

And thus began th' Exordivm of our woes,
the fatall dumbe shewe of our miserie:
Here sprang the tree on which our mischiefe growes,
the drery subiect of worlds tragedie.

Motto
Well, shepheard well, the golden age is gone,
Wishes may not reuoke that which is past:
It were no wit to make two griefes of one,
Our prouerb sayth, Nothing can alwayes last.

Listen to me my lovely shepheards joye,
And thou shalt heare with mirth and mickle glee,
A pretie Tale, which when I was a boy,
My toothles Grandame oft hath tolde to me.

Corbo
Shepheard say on, so may we passe the time,
There is no doubt it is some worthy ryme.

Motto
Farre in the countrey of Arden,
There wond a knight hight Cassemen,
As bolde as Isenbras:
Fell was he and eger bent,
In battell and in Tournament,
As was the good sir Topas.
He had as antique stories tell,
A daughter cleaped Dowsabell,
A may den fayre and free:
And for she was her fathers heire,
Full well she was ycond the leyre,
Of mickle curtesie.
The silke wel couth she twist and twine,
And make the fine Marchpine,
And with the needle werke,
And she couth helpe the priest to say

His Mattens on a holyday,
And sing a Psalme in Kirke.
She ware a frock of frolicke greene,
Might well be seeme a mayden Queene,
Which seemly was to see.
A hood to that so neat and fine,
In colour like the colombine,
Wrought full featuously.
Her feature all as fresh aboue,
As is the grasse that growes by Doue,
As lyth as lasse of Kent:
Her skin as soft as Lemster wooll,
As white as snow on peakish hull,
Or Swanne that swims in Trent.
This mayden in a morne betime,
Went forth when May was in her prime,
To get sweete Cerywall,
The hony-suckle, the Harlocke,
The Lilly and the Lady-smocke,
To deck her summer hall.
Thus as she wandred here and there,
picking of the bloomed Breere,
She chanced to espie
A shepheard sitting on a bancke,
Like Chanteclere he crowed crancke,
and pip'd with merrie glee:
He leard his sheepe as he him list,
When he would whistle in his fist,
to feede about him round:
Whilst he full many a caroll sung,
Untill the fields and medowes rung,
And that the woods did sound:
In fauour this same shepheards swayne,
Was like the bedlam Tamburlayne,
Which helde prowd Kings in awe:
But meeke he was as Lamb mought be,
Like that gentle Abel he,
Whom his lewd brother slaw.
This shepheard ware a sheepe gray cloke,
Which was of the finest loke,
That could be cut with sheere,
His mittens were of Bauzens skinne,
His cockers were of Cordiwin,
His hood of Meniueere.
His aule and lingell in a thong,
His tar-boxe on his broad belt hong,
His breech of Coyntrie blew:
Full crispe and curled were his lockes,

His browes as white as Albion rocks,
So like a lover true.
And pyping still he spent the day,
So mery as the Popingay:
Which liked Dowsabell,
That would she ought or would she nought,
This lad would never from her thought:
She in love-longing fell,
At length she tucked up her frocke,
White as the Lilly was her smocke,
She drew the shepheard nie,
But then the shepheard pyp'd a good,
That all his sheepe for sooke their foode,
To heare his melodie.
Thy sheepe quoth she cannot be leane,
That haue a iolly shepheards swayne,
The which can pipe so well.
Yea but (sayth he) their shepheard may,
If pyping thus he pine away,
In love of Dowsabell.
Of love fond boy take thou no keepe,
Quoth she, looke well vnto thy sheepe,
Lest they should hap to stray.
Quoth he, so had I done full well,
Had I not seene fayre Dowsabell,
Come forth to gather Maye.
With that she gan to vaile her head,
Her cheekes were like the Roses red,
But not a word she sayd.
With that the shepheard gan to frowne,
He threw his pretie pypes adowne,
And on the ground him layd.
Sayth she, I may not stay till night,
And leaue my summer hall vndight,
And all for long of thee.
My Coate sayth he, nor yet my foulde,
Shall neither sheepe nor shepheard hould,
Except thou fauour me.
Sayth she yet leuer I were dead,
Then I should lose my maydenhead,
And all for love of men:
Sayth he yet are you too vnkind,
If in your heart you cannot finde,
To love us now and then:
And I to thee will be as kinde,
As Colin was to Rosalinde,
of curtesie the flower:
Then will I be as true quoth she,

As euer mayden yet might be,
Unto her Paramour:
With that she bent her snow-white knee,
Downe by the shepheard kneeled shee,
And him she sweetely kist.
With that the shepheard whoop'd for joy,
Quoth he, ther's never shepheards boy,
That euer was so blist.

Gorbo

Now by my sheep-hooke here's a tale alone,
Learne me the same and I will giue thee hier,
This were as good as curds for our lone,
When at a night we sitten by the fire.

Motto

Why gentle hodge I will not sticke for that,
When we two meeten here another day,
But see whilst we haue set us downe to chat,
Yon tikes of mine begin to steale away.
And if thou wilt but come vnto our greene,
On Lammas day when as we haue our feast,
Thou shalt sit next vnto our summer Queene,
And thou shalt be the onely welcome guest.

THE NINTH EGLOG.

When cole-blacke night with sable vaile eclipsd the gladsome light,
Rowland in darkesome shade alone, bemoanes his wofull plight.

What time the wetherbeaten flockes,
Forsooke the fields to shrowd them in the folde,
The groues dispoyl'd of their fayre summer lockes,
The leaueles branches nipt with frostie colde,
The drouping trees their gaynesse all agone,
In mossie mantles doe expresse their moane.

When Phoebus from his Lemmans lovely bower,
Throughout the sphere had ierckt his angry lades,
His Carre now pass'd the heauens hie welked Tower,
Gan dragge adowne the occidentall slades,
In silent shade of desart all alone,
Thus to the night, Rowland bewrayes his moane.

Oh blessed starres which lend the darknes light,
The glorious paynting of that circled throane,

You eyes of heauen, you lanthornes of the night,
to you bright starres, to you I make my moane,
Or end my dayes, or ease me of my griefe,
The earth is frayle, and yeelds me no reliefe.

And thou fayre Phebe, cleerer to my sight,
Then Tytan is when brightest he hath shone,
Why shouldst thou now shut up thy blessed light,
And sdayne to looke on thy Endymion?
Perhaps the heauens me thus despight haue done,
Because I durst compare thee with their sunne.

If drery sighes the tempests of my brest,
Or streames of teares from floods of weeping eyes,
If downe-cast lookes with darksome cloudes opprest,
Or words which with sad accents fall and rise,
If these, nor her, nor you, to pittie moue,
There's neither helpe in you, nor hope in loue.

Oh fayr'st that lives, yet most vnkindest mayd,
O whilome thou the joy of all my flocke,
Why haue thine eyes these eyes of mine betrayd,
Unto thy hart more hard then flintie rocke,
And lastly thus depriu'd me of their sight,
From whome my love deriues both life and light.

Those dapper ditties pend vnto her prayse,
And those sweete straynes of tunefull pastorall,
She scorneth as the Lourdayns clownish layes,
And recketh as the rustick madrigall,
Her lippes prophane Ideas sacred name,
And sdayne to read the annals of her fame.

Those gorgeous garlands and those goodly flowers,
wherewith I crown'd her tresses in the prime,
She most abhors, and shuns those pleasant bowers,
made to disport her in the summer time:
She hates the sports and pastimes I inuent,
And as the toade, flies all my meriment.

With holy verses heryed I her glove,
And dew'd her cheekes with fountaines of my teares,
And carold her full many a lay of love,
Twisting sweete Roses in her golden hayres.
Her wandring sheepe full safely haue I kept,
And watch'd her flocke full oft when she hath slept.

Oenon never upon Ids hill,

So oft hath cald on Alexanders name,
As hath poore Rowland with an Angels quill,
erected trophies of Ideas fame:
Yet that false shepheard Oenon fled from thee,
I follow her that euer flies from me.

Ther's not a groue that wonders not my woe,
There's not a riuer weepes not at my tale:
I heare the ecchoes (wandring too and froe)
Resound my griefe in euery hill and dale,
The beasts in field, with many a wosull groane,
The birds in ayre help to expresse my moane.

Where been those lines? the heraulds of my heart,
my plaints, my tears, my vowes, my sighes, my prayers?
O what auayleth fayth, or what my Artes?
O love, ô hope, quite turn'd into despayres:
She stops her eares as Adder to the charmes,
And lets me lye and languish in my harmes.

All is agone, such is my endles griefe,
And my mishaps amended naught with moane,
I see the heauens will yeeld me no reliefe:
What helpeth care, when cure is past and gone,
And teares I see, doe me auayle no good,
But as great showres increase the rising flood.

With folded armes, thus hanging downe his head,
He gaue a groane as though his heart had broke,
Then looking pale and wan as he were dead,
He fetch'd a sigh, but never a word he spoke:
For now his heart wax'd cold as any stone,
Was never man aliue so woe begone.

With that fayre Cinthya stoups her glittering vayle,
And dives adowne into the Ocean flood,
The easterne brow which erst was wan and pale,
Now in the dawning blusheth red as blood:
The whistling Larke ymounted on her wings,
To the gray morrow, her good morrow sings.

When this poore shepheard Rowland of the Rocke,
Whose faynting legges his body scarse upheld,
Each shepheard now returning to his flocke,
Alone poore Rowland fled the pleasant field,
And in his Coate got to a vechie bed:
Was never man aliue so hard bested.

Michael Drayton was born in 1563, at Hartshill, near Atherstone, in Warwickshire.

He became a page to Sir Henry Goodere, at Polesworth Hall: his own words give the best picture of his early years here. His education would seem to have been good, but ordinary; and it is very doubtful if he ever went to a university. Besides the authors mentioned in the Epistle to Henry Reynolds, he was certainly familiar with Ovid and Horace, and possibly with Catullus: while there seems no reason to doubt that he read Greek, though it is quite true that his references to Greek authors do not prove any first-hand acquaintance. He understood French, and read Rabelais and the French sonneteers, and he seems to have been acquainted with Italian. His knowledge of English literature was wide, and his judgement good: but his chief bent lay towards the history, legendary and otherwise, of his native country, and his vast stores of learning on this subject bore fruit in the Poly-Olbion.

While still at Polesworth, Drayton fell in love with his patron's younger daughter, Anne; and, though she married, in 1596, Sir Henry Raynsford of Clifford, Drayton continued his devotion to her for many years, and also became an intimate friend of her husband's, writing a sincere elegy on his death.

About February, 1591, Drayton paid a visit to London, and published his first work, the Harmony of the Church, a series of paraphrases from the Old Testament, in fourteen-syllabled verse of no particular vigour or grace. This book was immediately suppressed by order of Archbishop Whitgift, possibly because it was supposed to savour of Puritanism. The author, however, published another edition in 1610; indeed, he seems to have had a fondness for this style of work; for in 1604 he published a dull poem, Moyses in a Map of his Miracles, re-issued in 1630 as Moses his Birth and Miracles. Accompanying this piece, in 1630, were two other 'Divine poems': Noah's Floud, and David and Goliath. Noah's Floud is, in part, one of Drayton's happiest attempts at the catalogue style of bestiary; and Mr. Elton finds in it some foreshadowing of the manner of Paradise Lost. But, as a whole, Drayton's attempts in this direction deserve the oblivion into which they, in common with the similar productions of other authors, have fallen. In the dedication and preface to the Harmony of the Church are some of the few traces of Euphuism shown in Drayton's work; passages in the Heroical Epistles also occur to the mind He was always averse to affectation, literary or otherwise, and in Elegy VIII deliberately condemns Lyly's fantastic style.

Probably before Drayton went up to London, Sir Henry Goodere saw that he would stand in need of a patron more powerful than the master of Polesworth, and introduced him to the Earl and Countess of Bedford. Those who believe Drayton to have been a Pope in petty spite, identify the 'Idea' of his earlier poems with Lucy, Countess of Bedford; though they are forced to acknowledge as self-evident that the 'Idea' of his later work is Anne, Lady Raynsford. They then proceed to say that Drayton, after consistently honouring the Countess in his verse for twelve years, abruptly transferred his allegiance, not forgetting to heap foul abuse on his former patroness, out of pique at some temporary withdrawal of favour. Not only is this directly contrary to all we know and can infer of Drayton's character, but Mr. Elton has decisively disproved it by a summary of bibliographical and other evidence. Into the question it is here unnecessary to enter, and it has been mentioned only because it alone, of the many Drayton-controversies, has cast any slur on the poet's reputation.

In 1593, Drayton published Idea, the Shepherds Garland, in nine Eclogues; in 1606 he added a tenth, the best of all, to the new edition, and rearranged the order, so that the new eclogue became the ninth. In these Pastorals, while following the Shepherds Calendar in many ways, he already displays something of the sturdy independence which characterized him through life. He abandons Spenser's quasi-rustic dialect, and, while keeping to most of the pastoral conventions, such as the singing-match and threnody, he contrives to introduce something of a more natural and homely strain. He keeps the political allusions, notably in the Eclogue containing the song in praise of Beta, who is, of course, Queen Elizabeth. But an over-bold remark in the last line of that song was struck out in 1606; and the new eclogue has no political reference. He is not ashamed to allude directly to Spenser; and indeed his direct debts are limited to a few scattered phrases, as in the Ballad of Dowsabel. Almost to the end of his literary career, Drayton mentions Spenser with reverence and praise.

It is in the songs interspersed in the Eclogues that Drayton's best work at this time is to be found: already his metrical versatility is discernible; for though he doubtless remembered the many varieties of metre employed by Spenser in the Calendar, his verses already bear a stamp of their own. The long but impetuous lines, such as 'Trim up her golden tresses with Apollo's sacred tree', afford a striking contrast to the archaic romance-metre, derived from Sir Thopas and its fellows, which appears in Dowsabel, and it again to the melancholy, murmuring cadences of the lament for Elphin. It must, however, be confessed that certain of the songs in the 1593 edition were full of recondite conceits and laboured antitheses, and were rightly struck out, to be replaced by lovelier poems, in the edition of 1606. The song to Beta was printed in Englands Helicon, 1600; here, for the first time, appeared the song of Dead Love, and for the only time, Rowlands Madrigal. In these songs, Drayton offends least in grammar, always a weak point with him; in the body of the Eclogues, in the earlier Sonnets, in the Odes, occur the most extraordinary and perplexing inversions. Quite the most striking feature of the Eclogues, especially in their later form, is their bold attempt at greater realism, at a breaking-away from the conventional images and scenery.

Having paid his tribute to one poetic fashion, Drayton in 1594 fell in with the prevailing craze for sonneteering, and published Ideas Mirrour, a series of fifty-one 'amours' or sonnets, with two prefatory poems, one by Drayton and one by an unknown, signing himself Gorbo il fidele. The title of these poems Drayton possibly borrowed from the French sonneteer, de Pontoux: in their style much recollection of Sidney, Constable, and Daniel is traceable. They are ostensibly addressed to his mistress, and some of them are genuine in feeling; but many are merely imitative exercises in conceit; some, apparently, trials in metre. These amours were again printed, with the title of 'sonnets', in 1599, 1600, 1602, 1603, 1605, 1608, 1610, 1613, 1619, and 1631, during the poet's lifetime. It is needless here to discuss whether Drayton were the 'rival poet' to Shakespeare, whether these sonnets were really addressed to a man, or merely to the ideal Platonic beauty; for those who are interested in these points, I subjoin references to the sonnets which touch upon them. From the prentice-work evident in many of the Amours, it would seem that certain of them are among Drayton's earliest poems; but others show a craftsman not meanly advanced in his art. Nevertheless, with few exceptions, this first 'bundle of sonnets' consists rather of trials of skill, bubbles of the mind; most of his sonnets which strike the reader as touched or penetrated with genuine passion belong to the editions from 1599 onwards; implying that his love for Anne Goodere, if at all represented in these poems, grew with his years, for the 'love-parting' is first found in the edition of 1619. But for us the question should not be, are these sonnets genuine representations of the personal feeling of the poet? but rather, how far do they arouse or echo in us as individuals the universal passion? There are at least some of Drayton's sonnets which possess a direct, instant, and universal appeal, by reason of their simple force and straightforward ring; and not in virtue of any subtle charm of sound and rhythm, or overmastering splendour of diction or thought. Ornament vanishes, and soberness and simplicity increase, as we proceed in the editions of the sonnets. Drayton's chief attempt in the jewelled or ornamental style appeared in 1595, with the title of Endimion and Phoebe, and was, in a sense, an imitation of Marlowe's Hero and Leander. Hero and Leander is, as Swinburne says, a shrine of Parian marble, illumined from within by a clear flame of passion; while Endimion and Phoebe is rather a curiously wrought tapestry, such as that in Mortimer's Tower, woven in splendid and harmonious colours, wherein, however, the figures attain no clearness or subtlety of outline, and move in semi-conventional scenery. It is, none the less, graceful and impressive, and of a like musical fluency with other poems of its class, such as Venus and Adonis, or Salmacis and Hermaphrodius. Parts of it were re-set and spoilt in a 1606 publication of Drayton's, called The Man in the Moone.

In 1593 and 1594 Drayton also published his earliest pieces on the mediaeval theme of the 'Falls of the Illustrious'; they were Peirs Gavesson and Matilda the faire and chaste daughter of the Lord Robert Fitzwater. Here Drayton followed in the track of Boccaccio, Lydgate, and the Mirrour for Magistrates, walking in the way which Chaucer had derided in his Monkes Tale: and with only too great fidelity does Drayton adapt himself to the dullnesses of his model: fine rhetoric is not altogether wanting, and there is, of course, the consciousness that these subjects deal with the history of his beloved country, but neither these, nor Robert, Duke of Normandy (1596), nor Great Cromwell, Earl of Essex (1607 and 1609), nor the Miseries of Margaret (1627) can escape the charge of tediousness. England's Heroical Epistles were first published in 1597, and other editions, of 1598, 1599, and 1602, contain new epistles. These are Drayton's first attempt to strike out a new and original vein of English poetry: they are a series of letters, modelled on Ovid's Heroides, addressed by various pairs of lovers, famous in English history, to each other, and arranged in chronological order, from Henry II and Rosamond to Lady Jane Grey and Lord Guilford Dudley. They are, in a sense, the most important of Drayton's writings, and they have certainly been the most popular, up to the early nineteenth century. In these poems Drayton foreshadowed, and probably inspired, the smooth style of Fairfax, Waller, and Dryden. The metre, the grammar, and the thought, are all perfectly easy to follow, even though he employs many of the Ovidian 'turns' and 'clenches'. A certain attempt at realization of the different characters is observable, but the poems are fine rhetorical exercises rather than realizations of the dramatic and passionate possibilities of their themes. In 1596, Drayton, as we have seen, published the Mortimeriados, a kind of epic, with Mortimer as its hero, of the wars between King Edward II and the Barons. It was written in the seven-line stanza of Chaucer's Troilus and Cressida and Spenser's Hymns. On its republication in 1603, with the title of the Barons' Wars, the metre was changed to ottava rima, and Drayton showed, in an excellent preface, that he fully appreciated the principles and the subtleties of the metrical art. While possessing many fine passages, the Barons' Wars is somewhat dull, lacking much of the poetry of the older version; and does not escape from Drayton's own criticism of Daniel's Chronicle Poems: 'too much historian in verse, ... His rhymes were smooth, his metres well did close, But yet his manner better fitted prose'. The description of Mortimer's Tower in the sixth book recalls the ornate style of Endimion and Phoebe, while the fifth book, describing the miseries of King Edward, is the most moving and dramatic. But there is a general lifelessness and lack of movement for which these purple passages barely atone. The cause of the production of so many chronicle poems about this time has been supposed to be the desire of showing the horrors of civil war, at a time when the queen was growing old, and no successor had, as it seemed, been accepted. Also they were a kind of parallel to the Chronicle Play; and Drayton, in any case even if we grant him to have been influenced by the example of Daniel, never needed much incentive to treat a national theme.

About this time, we find Drayton writing for the stage. It seems unnecessary here to discuss whether the writing of plays is evidence of Drayton's poverty, or his versatility; but the fact remains that he had a hand in the production of about twenty. Of these, the only one which certainly survives is The first part of the true and honorable historie, of the life of Sir John Oldcastle, the good Lord Cobham, &c. It is practically impossible to distinguish Drayton's share in this curious play, and it does not, therefore, materially assist the elucidation of the question whether he had any dramatic feeling or skill. It can be safely affirmed that the dramatic instinct was nor uppermost in his mind; he was a Seneca rather than a Euripides: but to deny him all dramatic idea, as does Dr. Whitaker, is too severe. There is decided, if slender, dramatic skill and feeling in certain of the Nymphals. Drayton's persons are usually, it must be said, rather figures in a tableau, or series of tableaux; but in the second and seventh Nymphals, and occasionally in the tenth, there is real dramatic movement. Closely connected with this question is the consideration of humour, which is wrongly denied to Drayton. Humour is observable first, perhaps, in the Owle (1604); then in the Ode to his Rival (1619); and later in the Nymphidia, Shepheards Sirena, and Muses Elyzium. The second Nymphal shows us the quiet laughter, the humorous twinkle, with which Drayton writes at times. The subject is an [Greek: agôn] or contest between two shepherds for the affections of a nymph called Lirope: Lalus is a vale-bred swain, of refined and elegant manners, skilled, nevertheless, in all manly sports and exercises; Cleon, no less a master in physical prowess, was nurtured by a hind in the mountains; the contrast between their manners is admirably sustained: Cleon is rough, inclined to be rude and scoffing, totally without tact, even where his mistress is concerned. Lalus remembers her upbringing and her tastes; he makes no unnecessary or ostentatious display of wealth; his gifts are simple and charming, while Cleon's are so grotesquely unsuited to a swain, that it is tempting to suppose that Drayton was quietly satirizing Marlowe's Passionate Shepherd. Lirope listens gravely to the swains in turn, and makes demure but provoking answers, raising each to the height of hope, and then casting them both down into the depths of despair; finally she refuses both, yet without altogether killing hope. Her first answer is a good specimen of her banter and of Drayton's humour.

On the accession of James I, Drayton hastened to greet the King with a somewhat laboured song To the Maiestie of King James; but this poem was apparently considered to be premature: he cried Vivat Rex, without having said, Mortua est eheu Regina, and accordingly he suffered the penalty of his 'forward pen', and was severely neglected by King and Court. Throughout James's reign a darker and more satirical mood possesses Drayton, intruding at times even into his strenuous recreation-ground, the Poly-Olbion, and manifesting itself more directly in his satires, the Owle (1604), the Moon-Calfe (1627), the Man in the Moone (1606), and his verse-letters and elegies; while his disappointment with the times, the country, and the King, flashes out occasionally even in the Odes, and is heard in his last publication, the Muses Elizium (1630). To counterbalance the disappointment in his hopes from the King, Drayton found a new and life-long friend in Walter Aston, of Tixall, in Staffordshire; this gentleman was created Knight of the Bath by James, and made Drayton one of his esquires. By Aston's 'continual bounty' the poet was able to devote himself almost entirely to more congenial literary work; for, while Meres speaks of the Poly-Olbion in 1598, and we may easily see that Drayton had the idea of that work at least as early as 1594, yet he cannot have been able to give much time to it till now. Nevertheless, the 'declining and corrupt times' worked on Drayton's mind and grieved and darkened his soul, for we must remember that he was perfectly prosperous then and was not therefore incited to satire by bodily want or distress.

In 1604 he published the Owle, a mild satire, under the form of a moral fable of government, reminding the reader a little of the Parlement of Foules. The Man in the Moone (1606) is partly a recension of Endimion and Phoebe, but is a heterogeneous mass of weakly satire, of no particular merit. The Moon-Calfe (1627) is Drayton's most savage and misanthropic excursion into the region of Satire; in which, though occasionally nobly ironic, he is more usually coarse and blustering, in the style of Marston. In 1605 Drayton brought out his first 'collected poems', from which the Eclogues and the Owle are omitted; and in 1606 he published his Poemes Lyrick and Pastorall, Odes, Eglogs, The Man in the Moone. Of these the Eglogs are a recension of the Shepherd's Garland of 1593: we have already spoken of The Man in the Moone. The Odes are by far the most important and striking feature of the book. In the preface, Drayton professes to be following Pindar, Anacreon, and Horace, though, as he modestly implies, at a great distance. Under the title of Odes he includes a variety of subjects, and a variety of metres; ranging from an Ode to his Harp or to his Criticks, to a Ballad of Agincourt, or a poem on the Rose compared with his Mistress. In the edition of 1619 appeared several more Odes, including some of the best; while many of the others underwent careful revision, notably the Ballad. 'Sing wee the Rose,' perhaps because of its unintelligibility, and the Ode to his friend John Savage, perhaps because too closely imitated from Horace, were omitted. Drayton was not the first to use the term Ode for a lyrical poem, in English: Soothern in 1584, and Daniel in 1592 had preceded him; but he was the first to give the name popularity in England, and to lift the kind as Ronsard had lifted it in France; and till the time of Cowper no other English poet showed mastery of the short, staccato measure of the Anacreontic as distinct from the Pindaric Ode. In the Odes Drayton shows to the fullest extent his metrical versatility: he touches the Skeltonic metre, the long ten-syllabled line of the Sacrifice to Apollo; and ascends from the smooth and melodious rhythms of the New Year through the inspiring harp-tones of the Virginian Voyage to the clangour and swing of the Ballad of Agincourt. His grammar is possibly more distorted here than anywhere, but, as Mr. Elton says, 'these are the obstacles of any poet who uses measures of four or six syllables.' His tone throughout is rather that of the harp, as played, perhaps, in Polesworth Hall, than that of any other instrument; but in 1619 Drayton has taken to him the lute of Carew and his compeers. In 1619 the style is lighter, the fancy gayer, more exquisite, more recondite. Most of his few metaphysical conceits are to be found in these later Odes, as in the Heart, the Valentine, and the Crier. In the comparison of the two editions the nobler, if more strained, tone of the earlier is obvious; it is still Elizabethan, in its nobility of ideal and purpose, in its enthusiasm, in its belief and confidence in England and her men; and this even though we catch a glimpse of the Jacobean woe in the Ode to John Savage: the 1619 Odes are of a different world; their spirit is lighter, more insouciant in appearance, though perhaps studiedly so; the rhythms are more fantastic, with less of strength and firmness, though with more of grace and superficial beauty; even the very textual alterations, while usually increasing the grace and the music of the lines, remind the reader that something of the old spontaneity and freshness is gone.

In 1607 and 1609, Drayton published two editions of the last and weakest of his mediaeval poems—the Legend of Great Cromwell; and for the next few years he produced nothing new, only attending to the publication of certain reprints and new editions. During this time, however, he was working steadily at the Poly-Olbion, helped by the patronage of Aston and of Prince Henry. In 1612-13, Drayton burst upon an indifferent world with the first part of the great poem, containing eighteen songs; the title-page will give the best idea of the contents and plan of the book: 'Poly-Olbion or a Chorographicall Description of the Tracts, Riuers, Mountaines, Forests, and other Parts of this renowned Isle of Great Britaine, With intermixture of the most Remarquable Stories, Antiquities, Wonders, Rarityes, Pleasures, and Commodities of the same: Digested in a Poem by Michael Drayton, Esq. With a Table added, for direction to those occurrences of Story and Antiquities, whereunto the Course of the Volume easily leades not.' &c. On this work Drayton had been engaged for nearly the whole of his poetical career. The learning and research displayed in the poem are extraordinary, almost equalling the erudition of Selden in his Annotations to each Song. The first part was, for various reasons, a drug in the market, and Drayton found great difficulty in securing a publisher for the second part. But during the years from 1613 to 1622, he became acquainted with Drummond of Hawthornden through a common friend, Sir William Alexander of Menstry, afterwards Earl of Stirling. In 1618, Drayton starts a correspondence; and towards the end of the year mentions that he is corresponding also with Andro Hart, bookseller, of Edinburgh. The subject of his letter was probably the publication of the Second Part; which Drayton alludes to in a letter of 1619 thus: 'I have done twelve books more, that is from the eighteenth book, which was Kent, if you note it; all the East part and North to the river Tweed; but it lies by me; for the booksellers and I are in terms; they are a company of base knaves, whom I both scorn and kick at.' Finally, in 1622, Drayton got Marriott, Grismand, and Dewe, of London, to take the work, and it was published with a dedication to Prince Charles, who, after his brother's death, had given Drayton patronage. Drayton's preface to the Second Part is well worth quoting:

'To any that will read it. When I first undertook this Poem, or, as some very skilful in this kind have pleased to term it, this Herculean labour, I was by some virtuous friends persuaded, that I should receive much comfort and encouragement therein; and for these reasons; First, that it was a new, clear, way, never before gone by any; then, that it contained all the Delicacies, Delights, and Rarities of this renowned Isle, interwoven with the Histories of the Britons, Saxons, Normans, and the later English: And further that there is scarcely any of the Nobility or Gentry of this land, but that he is in some way or other by his Blood interested therein. But it hath fallen out otherwise; for instead of that comfort, which my noble friends (from the freedom of their spirits) proposed as my due, I have met with barbarous ignorance, and base detraction; such a cloud hath the Devil drawn over the world's judgment, whose opinion is in few years fallen so far below all ballatry, that the lethargy is incurable: nay, some of the Stationers, that had the selling of the First Part of this Poem, because it went not so fast away in the sale, as some of their beastly and abominable trash, (a shame both to our language and nation) have either despitefully left out, or at least carelessly neglected the Epistles to the Readers, and so have cozened the buyers with unperfected books; which these that have undertaken the Second Part, have been forced to amend in the First, for the small number that are yet remaining in their hands. And some of our outlandish, unnatural, English, (I know not how otherwise to express them) stick not to say that there is nothing in this Island worth studying for, and take a great pride to be ignorant in any thing thereof; for these, since they delight in their folly, I wish it may be hereditary from them to their posterity, that their children may be begg'd for fools to the fifth generation, until it may be beyond the memory of man to know that there was ever other of their families: neither can this deter me from going on with Scotland, if means and time do not hinder me, to perform as much as I have promised in my First Song:

Till through the sleepy main, to Thuly I have gone,
And seen the Frozen Isles, the cold Deucalidon,
Amongst whose iron Rocks, grim Saturn yet remains
Bound in those gloomy caves with adamantine chains.

And as for those cattle whereof I spake before, Odi profanum vulgus, et arceo, of which I account them, be they never so great, and so I leave them. To my friends, and the lovers of my labours, I wish all happiness.
Michael Drayton.'

The Poly-Olbion as a whole is easy and pleasant to read; and though in some parts it savours too much of a mere catalogue, yet it has many things truly poetical. The best books are perhaps the XIII, XIV and XV, where he is on his own ground, and therefore naturally at his best. It is interesting to notice how much attention and space he devotes to Wales. He describes not only the 'wonders' but also the fauna and flora of each district; and of the two it would seem that the flowers interested him more. Though he was a keen observer of country sights and sounds (a fact sufficiently attested by the Nymphidia and the Nymphals), it is evident that his interest in most things except flowers was rather momentary or conventional than continuous and heart-felt; but of the flowers he loves to talk, whether he weaves us a garland for the Thame's wedding, or gives us the contents of a maund of simples; and his love, if somewhat homely and unimaginative, is apparent enough. But the main inspiration, as it is the main theme, of the Poly-Olbion is the glory and might and wealth, past, present, and future, of England, her possessions and her folk. Through all this glory, however, we catch the tone of Elizabethan sorrow over the 'Ruines of Time'; grief that all these mighty men and their works will perish and be forgotten, unless the poet makes them live for ever on the lips of men. Drayton's own voluminousness has defeated his purpose, and sunk his poem by its own bulk. Though it is difficult to go so far as Mr. Bullen, and say that the only thing better than a stroll in the Poly-Olbion is one in a Sussex lane, it is still harder to agree with Canon Beeching, that 'there are few beauties on the road', the beauties are many, though of a quietly rural type, and the road, if long and winding, is of good surface, while its cranks constitute much of its charm. It is doubtless, from the outside, an appalling poem in these days of epitomes and monographs, but it certainly deserves to be rescued from oblivion and read.

In 1618 Drayton contributed two Elegies to Henry FitzGeoffrey's Satyrs and Epigrames. These were on the Lady Penelope Clifton, and on 'the death of the three sonnes of the Lord Sheffield, drowned neere where Trent falleth into Humber'. Neither is remarkable save for far-fetched conceits; they were reprinted in 1610, and again, with many others, in the volume of 1627. In 1619 Drayton issued a folio collected edition of his works, and reprinted it in 1620. In 1627 followed a folio of wholly fresh matter, including the Battaile of Agincourt; the Miseries of Queene Margarite, Nimphidia, Quest of Cinthia, Shepheards Sirena, Moone-Calfe, and Elegies upon sundry occasions. The Battaile of Agincourt is a somewhat otiose expansion, with purple patches, of the Ballad; it is, nevertheless, Drayton's best lengthy piece on a historical theme. Of the Miseries of Queene Margarite and of the Moone-Calfe we have already spoken. The most notable piece in the book is the Nimphidia. This poem of the Court of Fairy has 'invention, grace, and humour', as Canon Beeching has said. It would be interesting to know exactly when it was composed and committed to paper, for it is thought that the three fairy poems in Herrick's Hesperides were written about 1626. In any case, Drayton's poem touches very little, and chiefly in the beginning, on the subject of any one of Herrick's three pieces. The style, execution, and impression left on the reader are quite different; even as they are totally unlike those of the Midsummer Night's Dream. Herrick's pieces are extraordinary combinations of the idea of 'King of Shadows', with a reality fantastically sober: the poems are steeped in moonlight. In Drayton all is clear day, or the most unromantic of nights; though everything is charming, there is no attempt at idealization, little of the higher faculty of imagination; but great realism, and much play of fancy. Herrick's verses were written by Cobweb and Moth together, Drayton's by Puck. Granting, however, the initial deficiency in subtlety of charm, the whole poem is inimitably graceful and piquant. The gay humour, the demure horror of the witchcraft, the terrible seriousness of the battle, wonderfully realize the mock-heroic gigantesque; and while there is not the minute accuracy of Gulliver in Lilliput, Drayton did not write for a sceptical or too-prying audience; quite half his readers believed more or less in fairies. In the metre of the poem Drayton again echoes that of the older romances, as he did in Dowsabel. In the Quest of Cinthia, while ostensibly we come to the real world of mortals, we are really in a non-existent land of pastoral convention, in the most pseudo-Arcadian atmosphere in which Drayton ever worked. The metre and the language are, however, charmingly managed. The Shepheards Sirena is a poem, apparently, 'where more is meant than meets the ear,' as so often in pastoral poetry; it is difficult to see exactly what is meant; but the Jacobean strain of doubt and fear is there, and the poem would seem to have been written some time earlier than 1627. The Elegies comprise a great variety of styles and themes; some are really threnodies, some verse-letters, some laments over the evil times, and one a summary of Drayton's literary opinions. He employs the couplet in his Elegies with a masterly hand, often with a deliberately rugged effect, as in his broader Marstonic satire addressed to William Browne; while the line of greater smoothness but equal strength is to be seen in the letters to Sandys and Jeffreys. He is fantastic and conceited in most of the threnodies; but, as is natural, that on his old friend, Sir Henry Raynsford, is least artificial and fullest of true feeling. The epistle to Henery Reynolds. Of Poets and Poesie shows Drayton as a sane and sagacious critic, ready to see the good, but keen to discern the weakness also; perhaps the clearest evidence of his critical skill is the way in which nearly all of his judgements on his contemporaries coincide with the received modern opinions.

In his later years Drayton enjoyed the patronage of the third Earl and Countess of Dorset; and in 1630 he published his last volume, the Muses Elizium, of which he dedicated the pastoral part to the Earl, and the three divine poems at the end to the Countess. The Muses Elizium proper consists of Ten Pastorals or Nymphals, prefaced by a Description of Elizium. The three divine poems have been mentioned before, and were Noah's Floud, Moses his Birth and Miracles, and David and Goliah. The Nymphals are the crown and summary of much of the best in Drayton's work. Here he departed from the conventional type of pastoral, even more than in the Shepherd's Garland; but to say that he sang of English rustic life would hardly be true: the sixth Nymphal, allowing for a few pardonable exaggerations by the competitors, is almost all English, if we except the names; so is the tenth with the same exception; the first and fourth might take place anywhere, but are not likely in any country; the second is more conventional; the fifth is almost, but not quite, English; the third, seventh, and ninth are avowedly classical in theme; while the eighth is a more delicate and subtle fairy poem than the Nymphidia. The fourth and tenth Nymphals are also touched with the sadder, almost satiric vein; the former inveighing against the English imitation of foreigners and love of extravagance in dress; while the tenth complains of the improvident and wasteful felling of trees in the English forests. This last Nymphal, though designedly an epilogue, is probably rather a warning than a despairing lament, even though we conceive the old satyr to be Drayton himself. As a whole the Nymphals show Drayton at his happiest and lightest in style and metre; at his moments of greatest serenity and even gaiety; an atmosphere of sunshine seems to envelope them all, though the sun sink behind a cloud in the last. His music now is that of a rippling stream, whereas in his earlier days he spoke weightier and more sonorous words, with a mouth of gold.

To estimate the poetical faculty of Drayton is a somewhat perplexing task; for, while rarely subtle, or rising to empyrean heights, he wrote in such varied styles, on such various themes, that the task, at first, seems that of criticizing many poets, not one. But through all his work runs the same eminently English spirit, the same honesty and clearness of idea, the same stolidity of purpose, and not infrequently of execution also; the same enthusiasm characterizes all his earlier, and much of his later work; the enthusiasm especially characteristic of Elizabethan England, and shown by Drayton in his passion for England and the English, in his triumphant joy in their splendid past, and his certainty of their future glory. As a poet, he lacked imagination and fine fury; he supplied their place by the airiest and clearest of fancies, by the strenuous labour of a great brain illumined by the steady flame of love for his country and for his lady. Mr. Courthope has said that he lacked loftiness and resolution of artistic purpose; without these, we ask, how could a man, not lavishly dowered with poetry in his soul, have achieved so much of it? It was his very fixity and loftiness of purpose, his English stubbornness and doggedness of resolution that enabled him to surmount so many obstacles of style and metre, of subject and thought. His two purposes, of glorifying his mistress and his friends, and of sounding England's glories past and future, while insisting on the dangers of a present decadence, never flagged or failed. All his poetry up to 1627 has this object directly or secondarily; and much after this date. Of the more abstract and universal aspects of his art he had not much conception; but he caught eagerly at the fashionable belief in the eternizing power of poetry; and had it not been that, where his patriotism was uppermost, he was deficient in humour and sense of proportion, he would have succeeded better: as it is, his more directly patriotic pieces are usually the dullest or longest of his works. He requires, like all other poets, the impulse of an absolutely personal and individual feeling, a moment of more intimate sympathy, to rouse him to his heights of song. Thus the Ballad of Agincourt is on the very theme of all patriotic themes that most attracted him; Virginian and other Voyages lay very close to his heart; and in certain sonnets to his lady lies his only imperishable work. Of sheer melody and power of song he had little, apart from his themes: he could not have sat down and written a few lark's or nightingale's notes about nothing as some of his contemporaries were able to do: he required the stimulus of a subject, and if he were really moved thereby he beat the music out. Only in one or two of the later Odes, and in the volumes of 1627 and 1630, does his music ever seem to flow from him naturally. Akin to this quality of broad and extensive workmanship, to this faculty of taking a subject and when writing, with all thought concentrated on it, rather than on the method of writing about it, is his strange lack of what are usually called 'quotations'. For this is not only due to the fact that he is little known; there are, besides, so few detached remarks or aphorisms that are separately quotable; so few examples of that curiosa felicitas of diction: lines like these,

Thy Bowe, halfe broke, is peec'd with old desire;
Her Bowe is beauty with ten thousand strings....

are rare enough. Drayton, in fact, comes as near controverting the statement Poeta nascitur, non fit, as any one in English literature: by diligent toil and earnest desire he won a place for himself in the second rank of English poets: through love he once set foot in the circle of the mightiest. Sincere he was always, simple often, sensuous rarely. His great industry, his careful study, and his great receptivity are shown in the unusual spectacle of a man who has sung well in the language of his youth, suddenly learning, in his age, the tongue spoken by the younger generation, and reproducing it with individuality and sureness of touch. It is in rhetoric, splendid or rugged, in argument, in plain statement or description, in the outline sketch of a picture, that Drayton excels; magic of atmosphere and colouring are rarely present. Stolidity is, perhaps, his besetting sin; yet it is the sign of a slow, not a dull, intellect; an intellect, like his heart, which never let slip what it had once taken to itself.

As a man Drayton would seem to have been an excellent type of the sturdy, clear-headed, but yet romantic and enthusiastic Englishman; gifted with much natural ability, sedulously increased by study; quietly humorous, self-restrained; and if temporarily soured by disappointment and the disjointed times, yet emerging at last into a greater serenity, a more unadulterated gaiety than had ever before characterized him. It is possible, but from his clear and sane balance of mind improbable, that many of his light later poems are due to deliberate self-blinding and self-deception, a walking in enchanted lands of the mind.

Of Drayton's three known portraits the earliest shows him at the age of thirty-six, and is now in the National Portrait Gallery. A look of quiet, speculative melancholy seems to pervade it; there is, as yet, no moroseness, no evidence of severe conflict with the world, no shadow of stress or of doubt. The second and best-known portrait shows us Drayton at the age of fifty, and was engraved by Hole, as a frontispiece to the poems of 1619. Here a notable change has come over the face; the mouth is hardened, and depressed at the corners through disappointment and disillusionment; the eyes are full of a pathos increased by the puzzled and perturbed uplift of the brows. Yet a stubbornness and tenacity of purpose invests the features and reminds us that Drayton is of the old and sound Elizabethan stock, 'on evil days though fallen.' Let it be remembered, that he was in 1613, when the portrait was taken, in more or less prosperous circumstances; it was the sad degeneracy, the meanness and feebleness of the generation around him, that chiefly depressed and embittered him. The final portrait, now in the Dulwich Gallery, represents the poet as a man of sixty-five; and is quite in keeping with the sunnier and calmer tone of his later poetry. It is the face of one who has not emerged unscathed from the world's conflict, but has attained to a certain calm, a measure of tranquillity, a portion of content, who has learnt the lesson that there is a soul of goodness in things evil. The Hole portrait shows him with long hair, small 'goatee' beard, and aquiline nose drawn up at the nostrils: while the National portrait shows a type of nose and beard intermediate between the Hole and the Dulwich pictures: the general contour of the face, though the forehead is broad enough, is long and oval. Drayton seems to have been tall and thin, and to have been very susceptible of cold, and therefore to have hated Winter and the North. He is said to have shared in the supper which caused Shakespeare's death; but his own verses breathe the spirit of Milton's sonnet to Cyriack Skinner, rather than that of a devotee of Bacchus.

He died in 1631, probably December 23, and was buried under the North wall of Westminster Abbey. Meres's opinion of his character during his early life is as follows: 'As Aulus Persius Flaccus is reported among al writers to be of an honest life and upright conuersation: so Michael Drayton, quem totics honoris et amoris causa nomino, among schollers, souldiours, Poets, and all sorts of people is helde for a man of uertuous disposition, honest conversation, and well governed cariage; which is almost miraculous among good wits in these declining and corrupt times, when there is nothing but rogery in villanous man, and when cheating and craftines is counted the cleanest wit, and soundest wisedome.' Fuller also, in a similar strain, says, 'He was a pious poet, his conscience having the command of his fancy, very temperate in his life, slow of speech, and inoffensive in company.'

A Chronology of Michael Drayton's Life and Works

1563	Drayton born at Hartshill, Warwickshire.
c. 1572	Drayton a page in the house of Sir Henry Goodere, at Polesworth.
c. 1574	Anne Goodere born
February, 1591	Drayton in London. Harmony of Church.
1593	Idea, the Shepherd's Garland. Legend of Peirs Gaveston.
1594	Ideas Mirrour. Matilda. Lucy Harrington becomes Countess of Bedford.
1595	Sir Henry Goodere the elder dies. Endimion and Phoebe, dedicated to Lucy Bedford.
1595-6	Anne Goodere married to Sir Henry Raynsford.
1596	Mortimeriados. Legends of Robert, Matilda, and Gaveston.
1597	England's Heroical Epistles.
1598	Drayton already at work on the Poly-Olbion.
1599	Epistles and Idea sonnets, new edition. (Date of Drayton portrait in National Portrait Gallery.)
1600	Sir John Oldcastle.
1602	New edition of Epistles and Idea.
1603	Drayton made an Esquire of the Bath, to Sir Walter Aston. To the Maiestie of King James. Barons' Wars.
1604	The Owle. A Pean Triumphall. Moyses in a Map of his Miracles.
1605	First collected edition of Poems. Another edition of Idea and Epistles.
1606	Poemes Lyrick and Pastorall. Odes. Eglogs. The Man in the Moone.
1607	Legend of Great Cromwell.
1608	Reprint of Collected Poems.
1609	Another edition of Cromwell.
1610	Reprint of Collected Poems.
1613	Reprint of Collected Poems. First Part of Poly-Olbion.
1618	Two Elegies in FitzGeoffrey's Satyrs and Epigrames.

1619	Collected Folio edition of Poems.
1620	Second edition of Elegies, and reprint of 1619 Poems.
1622	Poly-Olbion complete.
1627	Battle of Agincourt, Nymphidia, &c.
1630	Muses Elizium. Noah's Floud. Moses his Birth and Miracles. David and Goliah.
1631	Second edition of 1627 folio. Drayton dies December 23rd.
1636	Posthumous poem appeared in Annalia Dubrensia.
1637	Poems.

Michael Drayton – A Concise Bibliography

The Major Works

The Harmony of the Church (1591)
Idea, The Shepherd's Garland (1593)
Idea's Mirror (1594)
Peirs Gaveston (1593 or 1594)
Matilda (1594)
Endimion and Phoebe: Idea's Latmus (1595)
The Tragical Legend of Robert, Duke of Normandy (1596)
Mortimeriados (1596)
England's Heroicall Epistles (1597)
The First Part of the Life of Sir John Oldcastle (1600)
The Barons' Wars in the Reign of Edward II (1603)
The Owl (1604)
The Man in the Moon (1606)
The Legend of Thomas Cromwell, Earl of Essex (1607)
Poly-Olbion (1612 & 1622)
Idea (1619)
Pastorals: Containing Eclogues (1619)
Odes (1619)
The Battle of Agincourt (published 1627)
The Quest of Cynthia (published 1627)
Elegies Upon Sundry Occasions (1627)
Nymphidia, the Court of Fairy (1627)
The Shepherd's Sirena (1627)
Muses' Elysium (1630)
Moses' Birth and Miracles (1630)

www.ingramcontent.com/pod-product-compliance
Lightning Source LLC
Chambersburg PA
CBHW070110070426
42448CB00038B/2502